American Meth

American Meth

✦

A History of the Methamphetamine Epidemic in America

Sterling R Braswell

iUniverse, Inc.
New York Lincoln Shanghai

American Meth
A History of the Methamphetamine Epidemic in America

iUniverse books may be ordered through booksellers or by contacting:

iUniverse
2021 Pine Lake Road, Suite 100
Lincoln, NE 68512
www.iuniverse.com
1-800-Authors (1-800-288-4677)

ISBN-13: 978-0-595-38021-3 (pbk)
ISBN-13: 978-0-595-82392-5 (ebk)
ISBN-10: 0-595-38021-2 (pbk)
ISBN-10: 0-595-82392-0 (ebk)

Printed in the United States of America

Contents

Prologue

American Meth is about lunacy. More particularly, it is about a substance that makes lunatics out of the once sound-minded: the mechanic known to belly up to the bar for an hour before heading home, the hairdresser who always had a weakness, but rarely the money, for a line of cocaine. So often they are people who previously harbored normal appetites for the release recreational drugs and alcohol provide, only to lose all sense of restraint to a mysterious and alien influence. This is to say the typical user does not begin sinless, but neither is he or she necessarily born in single-minded pursuit of dissolution.

There is something inexplicably post-apocalyptic about the meth addict's existence. The color seems to have washed out of their world. As a former addict once put it, meth compels its user to "live like a coyote"—homeless, and constantly foraging for mere sustenance. But this coyote is, it should be remembered, a human being who once lived among family and friends in a house filled with things he or she owned.

This book is also about a very modern phenomenon, yet one with antecedents. Amphetamine was not first derived in the nineties at the dawn of the epidemic, as some might presume, but more than a century ago. Today methamphetamine is far and away the most prevalent synthetic drug clandestinely manufactured in the U.S. The trajectory is astonishing. In 1991 the DEA seized approximately 21 million dosage units of methamphetamine nationwide. The following year the number skyrocketed to 48 million. In 1996 more than 74 million units were seized, and the and in 2002 the number vaulted to an incredible 118 million dosage units. And they were seized in the most unlikely of places—the countryside. Here supplies are plentiful and meth manufacturers and dealers know small-town police are not ready for them. Turns out there is no safer haven than the bathtubs of doublewides tucked in amongst the verdant hills of southern Iowa, in machine shops on the edge of the scenic hamlets of eastern Kansas. And they have moved far beyond the Heartland, leaving in their wake a blight of insanity and violence that can only be described as cartoonlike.

In 1995 a man suffering from amphetamine psychosis broke into a San Diego National Guard armory and commandeered an unarmed Abrams tank. He then went on a rampage through residential neighborhoods, crushing cars, fire hydrants, anything that stood in his way. After taking the tank onto a freeway, he was finally stopped but refused to surrender, whereupon a police officer climbed atop the tank and shot the man through the heart.

Sixty miles to the north in Aguana a mobile home caught on fire after a mysterious explosion. According to witnesses at the scene, six or eight men ran out, fleeing for their lives, while outside the trailer a mother, holding her ten-year-old son, screamed that her other three children were still inside. When neighbors came running up to see if they could help, they were threatened by the men and warned away. No attempt was made to save the children, and when authorities arrived, the men scattered. Twelve hours later fire fighters waded through the charred remains to find the bodies of the three children, ages three, two, and one. The cause of the fire was determined to have been a methamphetamine lab explosion. When the men who had fled were finally rounded up, it was learned that they were not only meth "cooks" and dealers, but heavy users.

Paranoia is a hallmark of the meth user's lunacy. This is not the quaint and common form of the affliction whereby the neighbor lady thinks her phone is being tapped, but the eerily acute kind that causes users to become scared witless because they believe they are being chased by invisible spiders and plastic people. In their minds they have imaginary enemies by the score who are plotting and moving against them, and it is this quasi-reality, permeated with a scent of threat, that lends the meth culture its extraordinary violence. Remarkably few people fatally overdose on meth (only a few hundred in any given year out of millions of users); what kills is the paranoia it inspires. The meth addict feels his best friend is, other than meth itself, the automatic weapon.

But such an epidemic would not be possible were it not for recent extravagances in mainstream American culture at the command of the determined individual with access to boundless information. Though methamphetamine wasn't first derived here, it is a drug tailor made for a nation of do-it-yourselfers relentlessly drawn to the prospect of controlling time. Separatory funnels, Bunsen burners, molecular bits of synthetics, automatic weapons, cryptic formulae hardwired into the synapses of an electrified brain—these are the things that clutter the meth addict's life, all of which are harnessed by a combination of otherwise wholesome skills acquired in high school chemistry class and boot camp. A certain corner of the American psyche likes the idea of methamphetamine if not the reality.

This book is also a story about people who have lived in the drug's weird ether. To a certain extent it is my story, as it has cut a broad enough swath through my life that I feel uniquely qualified to expound upon it. In spite of this grim personal history, I would like to point out that I am not a prude when it comes to recreational drug use. Indeed, I have always been of the mind that, for many, life can be excruciatingly dull without something to give the day a little pop. But neither am I a flaming libertine who doesn't recognize a bad thing when he sees it.

Methamphetamine has been characterized by people who know as the greatest threat to a civilization ever posed by a drug. The threat is unique because the substance is unique. First, methamphetamine is extremely addictive. Experienced drug rehab workers say it's the hardest drug to kick they have ever come across, with ninety-five percent of the people who become addicted never able to quit. And there is a very specific reason for this. Meth operates at the most fundamental level of pleasure: in effect, it hijacks the body's biochemical reward system by priming the brain with the neurotransmitter dopamine, and then prevents its "reuptake," essentially keeping it from leaving the system. This is why a meth high lasts so many hours and days, instead of a few minutes or hours, typical of the effects of other drugs. Second, meth's effects on the body are often permanent, and include psychosis and severe depression. Of course some die by overdosing, and nothing is so permanent as death. Finally, and most terrifying of all, meth can be easily manufactured by the user, and even mutated into other drugs that produce a variety of effects. In essence, the user becomes the supplier, a kind of mom-and-pop pharmaceutical company. Within four or five hours anyone with the equipment, ingredients and a recipe (all of which are readily available) will have enough of the drug to impart a strong appetite to the inclined set at a quiet rural high school.

As with all recreational drugs, meth has spawned its own unique culture, one complete with jargon and folklore. Being inexpensive to manufacture it has become a favorite of the working poor, taking seed, as the stereotype would have it, in trailer parks and among the denizens of motorcycle gangs. Stereotypes of course are often little more than cruel exaggerations, but sometimes they contain a kernel of truth, or at least are not without substance. Like it or not, statistics bare out widely held preconceptions of methamphetamine culture. People arrested for manufacturing or possessing meth are overwhelmingly poor and white. They are also lacking in higher education, though the habit is gradually percolating up through the social-economic spectrum. The Hell's Angels have trafficked in the drug for decades, distributing yellow-white crystals nationwide in the black leather pannier bags of countless roaring Harleys. It is, as the condescending white-collar coke addict might say, the drug of choice among white trash.

What makes the story of amphetamine and methamphetamine so remarkable is the unprecedented nature of the epidemic itself. Civilized society cannot simply scorch meth where it grows as it would a poppy or pot field. Meth is an idea applied to a mixture of everyday things in our lives, things we cannot annihilate.

That leaves the idea, which is a famously hard thing to destroy, and meth is the cockroach in the animal kingdom of ideas.

And it is a very old idea. Over the past half-century amphetamines have drifted in and out of vogue, their popularity driven in unequal parts by the winds of fashion, youth culture, and necessity. Amphetamines have been a favorite of housewives, soldiers, working folks, students. In the main, it has been a drug favored by the industrious. But the aimless ways of youth culture have certainly held their sway.

Imagine the life and work of Jack Kerouac without the influence of Bennies. Similarly, the Mods of Britain darting off on their Italian scooters to seaside towns to rumble on bank holidays hardly seems likely without little pills they affectionately called Purple Hearts. The Northern Soul movement, also of Britain, combined amphetamine pill fare with a taste for exceedingly rare Motown forty-five records, and blended them into a very specific identity. Together, all of these micro-cultures, along with widespread use by mainstream American and European society, would foster the conditions necessary for the epidemic that was to come.

But unlike most drugs, meth has found an enthusiastic market among women. According to the Koch Crime Institute they are more likely to use methamphetamine than cocaine. There is a straight-forward theory accounting for this fact, as meth is by far the less expensive of the two central nervous system stimulants, as well as a great suppressor of appetite. Meth is renown for bringing a user's weight down in dramatic fashion, and has become evermore popular in an age that celebrates the sleek profile so assiduously. But there is another less direct theory worthy of consideration.

Speculation in certain quarters has it that both men and women who are drawn to meth may be so in part as a result of various pre-existing psychological conditions. Many female users suffer from a controversial condition called borderline personality disorder (BPD). People with BPD (seventy-five percent of whom are women) lead wildly chaotic personal lives, and have the peculiar inability to really "see" themselves moving through their lives from day to day, moment to moment, in any meaningful way. More specifically, they don't feel truly attached to the people around them, nor do they feel a part of the everyday ebb and flow of their own experience. Meth, however, may provide some temporary relief from the chaos of their tortured interior lives, allowing them—if only for a few hours—to feel intense personal attachment. Indeed, meth is something of a love drug.

But the story of amphetamine and methamphetamine (meth is amphetamine with a methyl molecule attached) begins in earnest at the dawn of the twentieth century with the military application of the drug. Amphetamine's primary martial value of course lay in its capacity to control, if only for a few days, the body clocks of fighting forces, an edge that has become of tactical necessity in modern warfare. Similarly, the current epidemic is a result of a civilian population that has become addicted to the momentary bliss this control provides. And that is the existential allure of meth: the illusion that one has conquered time itself.

Time is important not only to the psychic effect of the drug but to its rise in popularity. The history of meth is seamlessly connected to the present, and thus there is value in presenting the two simultaneously. By alternating a contemporary tale of amphetamine's veiled nature with the history of the drug itself, the epidemic can be seen in the immediate context of the forces that brought it to bear. And so our story begins close to home, with someone who was once very close to me…

Origins

1

When I saw Lucille in May of 1998 it was for the first time in thirteen years. The phone rang at my office earlier that day, and suddenly against my ear came the soft hum of her eerily familiar sing-song voice going on and on about how she was now living in Houston, freshly divorced, and working at an area medical clinic. There was something unhinged in her voice, a note of chumminess that sought to conceal the obvious fact that it had been a very long time. The forced attempt at the casual made the whole conversation a little impossible. After all these years, and out of the clear blue, she was wondering if maybe we could get together for dinner and drinks.

With my workday effectively arrested, I frittered away the remains of the afternoon drawing doodles on the numbered squares of my desk calendar, marking a grid of rows and columns of time, mentally organizing the past, wrapping my mind around thirteen years. In this way I prepared myself for the sight of Lucille.

And it was a necessary exercise. Looking across the table at her that night was to gaze backward across the chasm of adult life to the last gasp of a shared adolescence. We had been boyfriend and girlfriend in high school, lost our virginity together, got drunk for the first time together, skinny-dipped. Since then she'd become a physician's assistant while I had gotten rich in the recent technology boom. She was now a single mom; I'd spent the same period bouncing from one brief and absurd relationship to another. The intervening years, however, appeared to have weighed more heavily on Lucille: not too long ago a friend of hers in the medical profession had killed herself, and another had, just days before, lost her medical license for writing fraudulent prescriptions. Adulthood had shown itself to be a bit lonely for me but edging toward the ominous for her.

To my mind past and present are oddly difficult to distinguish when it comes to Lucille. Memories drift and run together. Perhaps this is because I never really stopped thinking of her during our thirteen-year hiatus, or perhaps because what she was and what she became are not all that far apart. The first time I ever laid eyes on her was in gym class during our junior year of high school. She was off by herself near the half-court line, dancing with her eyes closed while the other girls in her class played badminton. She was a lithe and nimble gymnast and dancer, shimmying, as she would in later years, to music only she could hear. She was self-assured but had very few girlfriends, and was, by all accounts, unusual except with respect to her interest in boys.

Our first date was an attempted escape from innocence—something like banana splits at Tastee Freeze followed by a secret foray over an oil tycoon's pool fence where we skinny-dipped without really touching. As we tread water, however, our noses inches apart and a ponderous moon overhead, I secured another date where something more was promised. Dustin, my best friend in high school, was house-sitting a sprawling mansion the following weekend, and I could get the keys. Lucille thought this a fine idea, as it would be her birthday, and she'd promised herself that the occasion would be marked by "significant events" throughout her life.

This second date involved a bottle of Chardonnay consumed in the master bedroom of this palatial home, coupled with an inadroit attempt at intercourse. But I was heartened by what seemed to be her native enthusiasm for all things sexual and by the fact that she agreed to a third date that involved her sneaking through my bedroom window. Many dates followed, which gradually came to instill in me the crude and naïve belief that all women were multi-orgasmic. Later I would come to realize that Lucille was different from most women in many ways.

A few days later I dropped by her house where I met her parents. I was raised with typical bourgeois Texas values, but Lucille, I could see from the outset, was brought up in very different circumstances among very different people. The first thing I took note of as I stepped from the car was her stepfather leaning against the sprung jamb of the screen door to their shabby ranch-style house, a bottle of Olympia resting upon the crown of a bulbous belly like a living caricature of the bitter stepfather. After the introductions, he began telling me how he'd been out of work for twelve years now, unable to get another job with the railroads. Lucille's mother wore a pillar of orange hair and smoked a Winston out on the stoop, rolling her hooded eyes, the lids of which were caked with blue eye shadow, as this man, her fourth husband, recited a familiar tale of economic misfortune. Bad vibes hung all about them and their place, and my business, as I saw it, was at home in my bedroom with Lucille. Guided by simple but true teenage instinct, I made a point of keeping a distance from that unhappy home.

We dated through what remained of high school, then one day Lucille told me of her plans to attend college in San Diego. I would be staying here in College Station, as my father worked for the A&M Ag Department, and my tuition would be free. After eighteen months of going steady, it had been a good go by high school standards, and by then we had both become distracted by our blossoming classmates. Prom was followed by graduation, which was followed by a summer of mutual but mild discontent. It didn't last long, for by August Lucille was gone. What I didn't know at the time was that she was escaping a ruined childhood.

About a week after she left her former neighbor stopped by my house to ask after Lucille. I'd seen him a few times before, but only in passing. He said he was happy to hear that she'd "gotten out of that house and away from that man," meaning, I assumed, any one of her many stepfathers.

The news made sense intuitively, even to my eighteen-year-old mind. On several occasions Lucille had made vague innuendo about slimy behavior by one of the "dirty old men" in her life. I never pressed her about what she meant by this and she never offered an explanation. Whatever happened, I figured it had something to do with what made her different from other girls our age. Ever since we'd been together her every thought seemed bent on the idea of escape—both psychological and physical. Now that she was gone, I could only assume she was happy.

We exchanged letters through our college careers as though propelled by habit and simple curiosity, but we saw each other only rarely. She transferred to another school and I pledged a fraternity. But there were happy surprises. In 1984 she called just before the Christmas holiday to say she was free for a few days and wanted to come up to College Station for a quick visit.

She arrived just as the town was getting laid low by a freakishly heavy snowstorm. The stately frat house, aglow in the snowy darkness, was completely empty save myself, and that night we carried on in bed and then called out for delivery. Her quick visit extended itself to three days of splendid solitude, but our relationship was in its final stage of evanescence. Once more she had to be going. Little did I know how many desk calendars I would scribble upon and discard before I saw her again.

In the wake of this final reunion, the letters I sent Lucille all came back. The letters I once received with regularity mysteriously stopped. And that was that. No more phone calls, no more contact. Total escape. Lucille became an elusive hologram, a vivid memory that lingered on and on. I always wondered what had become of her.

2

It is a drug with a history like no other. A favorite of an American president, a führer, of soldiers, poets, musicians, and madmen, its subtle presence limns the twentieth century in caricature, warping and fraying the edges of the historical picture.

Amphetamine was first synthesized in Germany two years before the birth of its most notorious proponent and addict, Adolph Hitler. In 1919 a Japanese pharmacologist developed a derivative of amphetamine by adding the methyl molecule, making methamphetamine for no useful purpose; it was simply more potent and easier to make than its parent drug. For thirty years the substance was in search of an ailment—until the late 1920s when it was discovered that this crystalline powder was useful in treating asthma, hay fever and depression. Being water-soluble it was ideal for injections. In 1932 the first amphetamine was marketed by the Smith Kline and French Company in the form of an over-the-counter inhaler. This was Benzedrine, a bronchial dilator designed for the treatment of respiratory congestion. The inhaler was a huge success, prompting the pharmacological community as a whole to come up with more than forty uses for the product. In 1937, for instance, it was found to be useful in treating narcolepsy, a spontaneous sleeping disorder.

That same year, amphetamine became available by prescription in tablet form. The American Medical Association's Council on Pharmacy and Chemistry noted that, "A feeling of exhilaration and sense of well-being was a consistent effect, and patients volunteered that there had been a definite increase in mental activity and efficiency."

But it was the bronchial inhaler that became the secret hit, one that would foretell the drug's broader future. By the lights of one study, each inhaler contained the equivalent of fifty-six amphetamine tablets. During the Great Depression people with no medical condition (such as jazz great Charlie Parker) found there was a pleasant, long-lasting high to be got by pulling off the nasal strips and dunking them in their coffee. Prohibition may have made the sale and consumption of alcohol illegal, but amphetamine was as legal as a glazed donut.

During this time the full spectrum of amphetamine's medical uses were slowly being revealed, and in some cases, invented. An obvious use was found relatively early on in treating obesity, as it simultaneously lays waste to the appetite and fires the metabolism. Near the end of the decade it was also found to help a certain category of unruly children who fared poorly in school. Though known to stimulate the central nervous system, children with what would come to be known as attention deficit hyperactivity disorder (ADHD) were actually calmed by small doses of the drug, and their ability to concentrate mysteriously improved.

Thus amphetamine and methamphetamine found their ailments. They also found the perfectly healthy fan, the recreational user among the down-and-out in a world growing ever bleaker. But it would not merely be an American drug. Amphetamine was a filament of pure light illuminating a globe on the brink of war. Among the ruins of the approaching Apocalypse it would establish for itself an entirely new role.

3

Lucille has been working at Weiss Clinic in Houston for but a few months when a doctor, an OBGYN, taps her on the shoulder and says her name. This is none other than Dustin, my friend from high school who had given us the keys to the mansion back in College Station all those years ago. He has only a minute or two to catch up, so the conversation pivots tightly around the immediate circumstances of how each came to be here in this hallway at this moment and what a small world it is after all. Then Dustin's beeper beeps. They smile and part ways, but before they are out of earshot Lucille calls down the hall, "You wouldn't know whatever happened to Sterling, would you?"

A peculiar future hinges upon this rather ordinary moment. Little can anyone guess, of course, what kind of the future it will be.

A few days later comes Lucille's call, and that night we go out to the Capital Grill for dinner and drinks. She looks remarkably unchanged. A faint set of crow's feet set into the temples, but otherwise the same young Lucille with a vengeance. The transformation lies in her personality. The confident school girl now has a bashful side. Every now and then, however, she breaks out with a bawdy joke told in a loud Texas twang. Surrounding tables turn their heads in pleasant surprise, and then mild dismay. At this point she catches herself. Her voice is quieted, her gestures carefully trimmed. The picture she presents in that moment charms: the outburst is succeeded by an act of self-restraint employed, one suspects, at the bidding of hard-won wisdom. She has endured difficult times and emerged slightly touched—but with a transcendent self-awareness. Even in the midst of the outburst, I am a captive and unembarrassed audience. Lucille is my past. She is me.

The night ends on a note of innocence reminiscent of years gone by when I drop her off at her apartment. A peck on the cheek, and it's back to the car. The following weekend we go to a shindig hosted by Mark Cuban and his company Micro Solutions at Lake Conroe, just north of Houston. The parking lot is bumper-to-bumper BMWs and Audis, the party in full swing. Music pours out onto the lawn where blue smoke from a huge grill spirals over the lake. I ferry Lucille from cloister to cloister, introducing her to the people I've worked with pretty much since I saw her thirteen years ago. She seems perfectly comfortable in this company until I intimate how much money some of these people are worth. Suddenly the party is no longer a gathering of friendly computer gnomes, but a summit of movers and shakers, a party of young princes. At the first sign of swagger, Lucille retreats. She drifts into corners and vacant hallways, sipping her drink alone.

By late afternoon we have to be going, as Lucille's baby sitter has plans of her own that night. On the way to her place, Lucille says she needs to stop by a pharmacy to pick up a prescription for her migraines, so she asks me for the phone and puts in a call to her neighborhood Texas Drugmart. She tells the pharmacist she'll be there to pick it up in ten minutes.

"You can call in your own prescriptions just like that?" I ask once she hangs up.

"I'm in the industry," she says equably.

"That's too convenient," I say. "See, I'd be a fiend within a week."

In the long silent moment that follows I am left to believe she doesn't appreciate even the slightest implication that might impugn her capacity for self-control and therefore her professionalism. And I can understand that. Nobody dies when I mess up at work. Then in a horrible instant I recall the circumstances of her friend's trouble. I am a fool…

As we come into her neighborhood she silently directs me to the pharmacy. I drop her off before the sliding doors, and five minutes later she's smiling with mock relief, holding up to the sunlight a translucent pear-shaped nasal inhaler as she approaches the car. Once in the car she takes a couple of toots, and everything is fine, the menacing apparition in her brain subdued.

We then head to her apartment where I see her daughter, Emily, for the first time. The moment is mind-blowing for me, but privately so. The first view is common enough. Emily paws at the arm of the babysitter who doesn't want to be bothered. The babysitter is a young girl with acne and stringy black hair, absently clicking through endless cable channels. The conversation I'm having with myself can be condensed down to: Great God Almighty, Lucille has a daughter.

The instant the little girl notices us she ambles into Lucille's arms as the babysitter recites the afternoon's events. Nothing much happened and she wants her money. Lucille produces a couple of twenties from her purse, and the girl is out of there.

The balance of the afternoon is spent on the floor before the colorful glow of cartoons and children's shows. Kiddie banter breaks up long stretches of songs sung by demented adults. Just as I think it might be time for me to be going, Lucille asks if I'd like a bourbon and Coke. You bet.

She pours two drinks, then decides it's time to put Emily to bed. Once that's accomplished, we stretch out, and evening fades into night right there on the living room floor. At some point we make it to the bedroom where Lucille quickly ebbs into sleep. I lie awake beside her, thinking, my mind tumbling on and on.

I contemplate probabilities…how unlikely the last few days seem, the chances of Lucille and me getting back together like this after all these years. I think of how right it feels, how it all must have been orchestrated by some mysterious force, how reunions can seem to be coerced by the hand of God Himself. Lucille lays beside me, still as a mummy, the house filled with the scent of baby powder and a diaper pale somewhere in the darkness, past and present all mixed together in this one moment. I feel as though I've been rescued from the intolerable torpor of a former daily life, a dulling routine of work and stale weekend hi-jinx with coworkers and a coterie of friends who go way, way back, but never so far back as Lucille and me.

And now, with halting suddenness, the future stretches out before me in a succession of sunny vistas. It's the suddenness that keeps me awake. Such vistas that come late at night are notoriously unreliable. Fantasy intrudes upon reality in the wee hours.

Filament of Pure Light

4

The role amphetamines would play in the Second World War was based, either directly or indirectly, on preliminary studies conducted by various pharmaceutical companies that showed the drug could enhance intellectual performance by elevating wakefulness. Further research conducted by both the Allied and Axis militaries showed it also increased aggression. This wasn't a revved-up form of coffee, but something very different. From the battlefields of the South Pacific to the skies over London and Berlin, to the führerbunker where Hitler would spend his last days—the drug was everywhere. Indeed, amphetamine was the soul of this new kind of hyper-mobilized warfare, the very essence of *blitzkrieg*.

It isn't an exaggeration to say that amphetamine may have altered the history of the twentieth century, for there are a few remarkable albeit little-known facts regarding its role that lie at the doorstep of the century's central atrocity, the Holocaust.

Beginning in October of 1942, Adolph Hitler received daily injections of amphetamine from his personal physician, Dr. T. Morell, injections that gradually increased over time, impairing what was already precarious judgment. The significance of this timeframe lies in the fact that the injections coincided with the stoking of the first fires at concentration camps across Eastern Europe. This is to say that the massive scope and madness of Hitler's "final solution" may have been fueled to some degree by a steady stream of this crystalline powder. The degree, however, is open to speculation.

According to the National Parkinson Foundation, Morell gave these injections in an inept attempt at treating what is now believed to have been symptoms of Hitler's Parkinson's disease. As can be seen in various film footage, tremors began to shake the left side of Hitler's body as early as 1940. The tremors first appeared in his left arm, and then later in his left leg. He also incurred other classic symptoms of Parkinson's, developing gravely, unintelligible speech patterns, a left leg that he had to drag, and an unchanging, zombie-like facial expression.

The first symptoms were apparent as early as 1934 in Leni Reifenstahl's film "Triumph of the Will," which was made in Nuremburg during the Second Annual Nazi Party Congress when Hitler was forty-five years old. In the film the movement of Hitler's left arm appears severely limited, as he keeps it clamped against his side. By the autumn of 1942, when the tremors became noticeable to those around him, he was fifty-three, and was taking a whole host of drugs thought to calm such tremors and treat fatigue, depression and anxiety. His daily diet of drugs included Dalmann tablets (which contain caffeine), Brom-Nervacit, and methamphetamine—all of which, ironically, would only increase his tremor.

Of course the Nazis' assault on European Jews predated Hitler's use of methamphetamine. As Daniel Jonah Goldhager puts it in his book Hitler's Willing Executioners, "Hitler opted for genocide at the first moment that the policy became practical." We know much of how his mind worked, as he documented the development of his political thinking in *Mein Kampf*, written in 1924 while imprisoned at Landsberg after a failed putsch. Published shortly after his release, the memoir lays bare a blue-print for the coming cataclysm in which Germany would dominate the continent by pushing eastward for *lebensraum*, or living space. Thus, as Hitler came to power, he was by-and-large simply doing what he said he would do. Following this logic it would be an overstatement to characterize Krystalnacht as a carefully calibrated act of terror and the horror that followed as a mere methamphetamine-inspired rampage.

And yet there is a difference between the relatively small-time terror of Krystalnacht intended largely for political ends, and following through with the systematic slaughter of six million human beings. On January 20, 1942, German officials gathered at Wannsee, a suburb of Berlin, to discuss the final destruction of European Jewry. Before what became known as the Wannsee Conference, the solution to the Jewish question was less final, being more of the tenor of Krystalnacht. After the conference it was *most* final, with new concentration camps going up in Belzec, Sobibor, and Treblinka.

Also of great significance is the aspect of what the decision to enact this policy of systematic mass slaughter meant for Hitler personally: it was not only homicidal but suicidal. By initiating his final solution he surely knew that he either had to win the war or die—and by January of 1942 America, the world's greatest industrial power, was an enemy combatant. To military observers the tide of the war had turned unmistakably and irrevocably against Hitler. On the surface it would seem that the decision reached at Wannsee was a needlessly cruel and insane raising of the stakes as it made far less likely, if not impossible, the idea of Germany suing for peace. Without this option Hitler's very survival was made less likely if not impossible. In kind, having methamphetamine injected into your arm daily would seem to explain a lot.

Although methamphetamine is water-soluble and therefore very "injectable," doing so is, according to the *Consumer Report on Licit and Illicit Drugs*, "among the most disastrous forms of drug use yet devised." The high is nearly instanta-neous and wildly intense. It is also a very long way down when the effect of the drug wears off. During this period of withdrawal (now commonly known as "tweaking"), the user is typically prone to violence, delusions, and acute paranoia. All of these behaviors are hallmarks of Hitler's mindset as the war came to its apocalyptic conclusion on the European continent.

Again, it is possible to overstate the effect these daily injections had on Hitler's judgment and therefore the course of history. This is due to the simple fact that he was violent, delusional and paranoid long before Dr. Morell found the first vein in Hitler's forearm. But from that moment on Hitler was also suicidal.

5

My friends arrive at the ranch in the late morning on the third of July in pairs, and then three at a time, for a few days of holiday celebration. I intend to show off Lucille and the big spread. A stock pond sits behind its earthen dike, full of bass and catfish, surrounded by walnut trees. Gleaming new fence-line rings a newly acquired sixty acres. And presiding over it all is a small house, furnished and decorated with things like teak coffee tables and twenty-dollar-per-square-foot maple floors—the jewel at the center of an engagement ring waiting to be presented.

Mine is a life that, after thirty-five years, has come to fruition. Or so I would like it to appear even from the most intimate proximities. I have a house in a ritzy Houston neighborhood, and this ranch. A Jaguar XK8 gets me between the two, and a thriving career pays for it all. I do not yet have, as the unlucky say, much of a story to tell.

By eleven Greg and Earl, two friends from college, are seated on the back porch overlooking a hardwood grove. We're drinking bourbon on the rocks, talking, watching the sun's ascent. Eventually Lucille joins us, and the conversation becomes rollickingly convivial, and I am sitting here thinking, This is too good to be true. All of the elements in life that I love assembled in one moment, and the measured, amiable progression of time in which into enjoy it all.

By noon Laura and her husband Randy arrive. I fire up the grill, turn up the stereo, open the windows, and the celebration is in full swing. We fish along the banks of the pond, cruise through the woods on four-wheelers, drinks in hand. That night everyone goes to bed face down and snookered, and in the morning the house is roused by the sound of Laura churning out bloody Marys by the quart in the blender. By the second afternoon, the Fourth of July, the party seems to be buckling under the weight of the sourmash. The fishing rods lay abandoned by the pond, the four-wheelers are randomly nosed up to the house. I take some time myself to put down the glass and escape to the cool interior of my bedroom.

The sleep is brief and restless, burdened as I am with obligations of host. I get up in short order and wander out to the backyard where I find everyone lounging on the lawn furniture, laying on the grass, or sitting up, eyes drawn to the same incredible scene. Laura stands with her back to Lucille, Laura's summer dress hiked up around her waist, the blonde panty lines exposed to a hypodermic needle and plunger poised against Lucille's thumb.

"Lucille's giving me something for my hangover," Laura casually explains, winking and then wincing just as Lucille stabs her buttocks and depresses the plunger.

Lucille's eyes are momentarily wide with concentration. As she withdraws the syringe, she says to Laura in a very motherly tone, "Now lie down and relax." And Laura wanders off to a bedroom, following Lucille's instructions like a good little girl. Once she's gone, Lucille turns to everyone and asks, "Anyone else not feeling up to snuff?"

So everyone lines up, unbuckling belts and exposing the crests of their buttocks to receive the inoculation. When they're through, they all do as Lucille says and retire. Soon the house is full of my resting friends.

"So what was in the shot?" I ask once we're alone.

"A cocktail," Lucille says as though such an injection were common as a gin and tonic.

"A cocktail of what?"

Bringing her arms around my neck, she says, "Something safe and legal."

"Needles make me nervous."

She gently bites her lip. "I should have asked you first."

I shrug a little anxiously.

"Remember: safe and legal," she adds.

"Safe and legal are good."

"Please don't worry."

"What can I say? I'm a worrier."

And that is that. Lucille says she needs to follow her own advice, and off she goes.

In the meantime I wander from room to room, surreptitiously making sure everyone is doing all right. An hour or so later Lucille's patients emerge, one at a time, looking remarkably refreshed. Laura appears first. She stands before me on the lawn, blinking as if in disbelief at the clarity of her own senses, and says, "Oh my god...I feel...*incredible*..."

"Bet you've never been to a party like this before," I say with a measure of relief.

She turns her gaze to the window and smiles secretly.

"You provide the hangover," she says, "Lucille the cure."

When Randy, Greg and Earl finally emerge the verdict is the same. Lucille is Dr. Fix-it. This seems to have a decisive effect on Laura's thinking. As I head for the bar to refresh her drink, she says to me, "Lucille is *so sweet*, Sterling. Definitely a keeper."

There's sincerity, even earnestness, in the remark. And a realization begins to dawn on me. I need to lighten up, perhaps embrace this vaguely illicit element Lucille has brought into my life. Excessive orderliness should give way to this precisely calibrated mode of fun where any potential for mishap is held at bay by laminated medical credentials. Grown-up antics among responsible adults. A professionally guided tour through a funhouse. If only I knew then what I know now.

Once the sun is down I set up a fireworks display. The partying recommences as the thick fuses are lit and the rockets furiously rush into the night sky. Lucille silently approaches from behind and takes my hand in hers. I squeeze her palm and the pressure is returned. She pulls me about to face her.

"And how are you, my dear?" I say as the twin reflections of firework patterns blossom and float over the glossy lenses of her eyes.

"Never better…" And then she kisses me in such a way that makes me believe her implicitly.

Carried Aloft on Glow-in-the-Dark Clouds

6

Amphetamines were not the sole domain of madmen holed-up in bunkers during World War II. Allied and Axis forces alike knew the benefits of making the drugs available to their fighting men, but none applied the drug's singular traits to combat so effectively as the Japanese.

The germ of a new and murderously radical idea was planted long ago. In 1281 Japan was about to be devoured by the massive Mongol army led by none other than Genghis Khan. But nature would intervene in a way no one would ever forget. As Japan awaited its destruction an enormous typhoon struck the island nation, wiping out the greater part of the invading force. Japan had been saved. Unable to explain their good fortune, the Japanese called the typhoon the Divine Wind, or *Kamikaze*.

Seven centuries later, in the autumn of 1944, Japan found itself in similar straits. Instead of the Mongols, this time it was the armed forces of the United States bearing down, and a typhoon would only delay the inevitable. In a desperate attempt to stem the tide of war, the Japanese turned back to history to revive the memory of the Kamikaze.

The historical allusion was a legend wrapped in a euphemism for a suicide mission to be carried out by the country's most impressionable and compliant, its teenage boys. These young men and their bomb-loaded airplanes would be the world's first "smart" bombs. The tactic was developed by, among others, Japanese Vice Admiral Takashiro, who noted the destructive power of an airplane crashing into a ship. Packed with a half-ton of explosives, it could cripple an aircraft carrier, strip the deck of aircraft, or send a cruiser into salty oblivion. All that was needed were pilots eager to die for their Emperor.

There would be no shortage. Thousands volunteered, far more than the Japanese military planners had aircraft. The Kamikaze pilot was typically recruited in his late teens and assured that by fulfilling his mission he would save the empire in its darkest hour just as the Divine Wind had seven centuries earlier. Before and after a solemn ceremony with a kind of communion with sake, the pilot was injected with heavy doses of liquid methamphetamine known by the pharmaceutical brand name of *Philopon*. He then climbed into his bomb-laden plane for launch on his lonely one-way mission. Total commitment on the part of the pilot was the key.

The concept of the suicide mission as part of a broad military strategy horrified the American public. The bewildering nature of the attacks were utterly foreign to Western ideas on how civilized nations conducted themselves even in the murderous dementia of war. The American G.I. signed up for the dangerous mission, not the suicide mission. Even the Nazis were unwilling to sacrifice their lives so flagrantly for their führer.

To be sure the mentality of the Kamikaze pilot had much to do with the process of indoctrination visited upon him at such an impressionable age. But the Japanese leadership clearly knew what they were doing by ginning up young conscripts on methamphetamine so that they arrived in that most singular frame of mind when their target came into view. All the young Kamikaze had to do was, literally, to become one with it.

The suicide mission wasn't the only application of the drug during the Second World War. This was a war fought by men who were, by necessity, vividly alert. From the beginning it proved to be a new kind of fighting, a war characterized by the mobility of massive forces, fluid fronts, and radical innovations in weaponry. Amphetamines fit into this milieu perfectly, as they facilitated a new sharpness of mind, an alertness not required of troops in The Great War who slogged through a war of attrition. Pale-faced soldiers burrowing into the static mud of Flanders had given way to lightning aerial strikes on European and Asian capitals, and bulging fronts that morphed with the passing of hours.

Through the summer and fall of 1940 England fought alone for its very survival by scrambling squadrons of Spitfire and Hurricane fighters over southern England to meet waves of German bombers lumbering toward Whitehall and Buckingham Palace. But England was at a severe disadvantage, having precious few aircraft and qualified pilots after the long debilitating process of appeasement of the thirties. To make up for the deficit of pilots, squadrons were required to fly two, three, and sometimes four sorties each day. So grueling was the routine that pilots often fell asleep in-flight or immediately after landing. Sleep, as much as skilled pilots, was in short supply.

The head of Fighter Command, Air Chief Marshal Sir Hugh Dowding, understood that sleep and pilots were to some extent interchangeable. That is, more could be got out of each pilot if a measure of control over the body clock could be achieved. A central nervous system stimulus, he was advised, could provide that control. Without hesitation, seventy-three million amphetamine tablets, in the form of Benzedrine ("Bennies") and Benzedrine inhalers were made readily available. When pilots needed to sleep, they may or may not be able to sleep. But when they needed to be not only awake but alert, they would surely be capable of tearing a hole in the sky.

All the while, on the far side of the globe, tremendous stockpiles of Philopon were being built up to bolster the efforts of Kamikaze pilots and Japanese soldiers running wild in the jungles and islands of the Pacific Theatres. But as the Imperial military faltered and the armies retreated to the home islands, two unprecedented explosions brought an unexpectedly abrupt end to the fighting. No one could have predicted the nature of the hell that was about to occur under the soaring mushroom clouds of Hiroshima and Nagasaki. Nor could they have known that the stage was now set for the first amphetamine crisis in the history of the world.

7

Hot black Louisiana coffee can't rouse Lucille. A lethargic morning spent before the television, and she needs a nap. So the day is abandoned before it really begins.

She picks up Emily who has been awake since dawn and carries her into the bedroom where the blinds are drawn against the blazing late-summer sun and the brittle sound of insect wings hovering in the hot air. While they sleep I head down the winding lane where my ranch hand inches the bulldozer over the crown of a second earthen dike.

Diesel exhaust pours across the pond surface as the blade leavens the gravely soil into a shallow grade. The dike looks just as it did when I was here three weeks ago over the Fourth of July weekend. Continuing on I come across the shed where we store supplies and equipment such as fish food, post-hole diggers and bailing twine. A huge nickel-plated padlock I've never seen before hangs from the door latch. Heading down the lane a little further I see someone has set up a perch in a pin oak. A brickglass ashtray bristling with cigarette butts rests precariously between two branches. On the ground below shell casings are scattered.

I head over to Clyde who's riding the dozer kind of sidesaddle, like it was a horse. A cigarette juts from the corner of his mouth, a filthy plastic mesh International Harvester cap pulled down hard over his small pale head. The moment he sees me, he casually kills the engine and hops down.

"Howdy, Mr. Braswell," he says with a smile that exposes a rictus of abominable dental work. "Been putting the finishing touches on the dike for the past couple of weeks."

"Doesn't look any different than the last time I was here," I say.

Clyde averts his gaze to the hazy distance.

"Haven't been able to work because I haven't been paid."

"I paid you two weeks ago."

"And I'm been busting a hump ever since."

I shake my head at this nonsequitur and ask about the lock on the shed.

"Gonna re-seed the hayfield," he says.

"That's what's in the shed? Hay seed?"

"Yessir."

With this display of initiative all is forgiven.

"Come on over to the house when you're done, and I'll cut you another check," I say.

He climbs back into the dozer and I head into the woods by the house to collect firewood for a bonfire this evening. After an hour or two of work, I hear Lucille and Emily stirring about the house. The moment I come inside I can tell Lucille still isn't rested. Her eyes are swollen and she's entirely out of sorts.

"I feel a migraine coming on," she says, tears glazing her eyes in fearful dread of what lay in store. "Could you get my purse, baby?"

While I'm looking about, Clyde appears at the sliding door. Lucille hurls it open whereupon Clyde calls across the living room for his check.

"Be right with you, Clyde," I say with mounting panic as Lucille now has her thumbs pressed into her temples. Clyde's presence—his sweaty sleeveless t-shirt exposing a deep farmer's tan—is about to pitch her over the edge. Alas, I find her purse, pull out the inhaler, and toss it to Lucille.

"Oh, honey, it's empty," she says, her voice a plaintive bawl. "I'll need a refill."

"Call one in to the Walgreens in town and I'll pick it up."

Lucille rummages for the phone through the clutter on the counter as Clyde says confidentially, "Got a nasty headache, do you?"

Lucille nods spastically. Meanwhile, I'm out the door and making a beeline for the car, leaving Clyde to look after my girl while I'm gone.

Town is five winding miles away. The pharmacist has to answer the phone a couple of times before he can fill the prescription, but I'm back at the ranch within half an hour. When I come through the door, Lucille has the stereo on and is dancing before the full-length mirror in the bedroom. Through the window I can see Clyde is back on the dozer, a rooster tail of black exhaust bursting over the treetops, apparently ready to put in his first full day of work in a couple of weeks.

"Feeling better?" I ask Lucillle as I come up behind her in the bedroom.

"The mystery of migraines…sort of evaporated after you left."

I hand her the refilled prescription, and she shimmies her way over to her purse and stows it away.

"So what do you think of Clyde?" I ask.

"Lord, what a *sweet*-heart, Sterling," she says coming into my arms. "I didn't know people like that walked the earth."

8

As the twin radioactive columns drifted into the jet stream, a devastated Japanese population staggered to its feet from the ashes of a four-year war.

But not all of Japan's matériel had been destroyed. For example, the enormous stockpile of Philopon was still intact. In the months after the war cash-strapped pharmaceutical companies sold off their vast supplies to the general public who eagerly lost themselves in an amphetamine dream to escape a nuclear reality that included something horrible and new—tens of thousands of people dying of radiation exposure. The pharmaceutical companies' most avid customers tended to be young veterans and juveniles, the most disillusioned of the most deeply disoriented population in the history of the civilized world. But the price for this business would be paid sooner rather than later. According to records of the Japanese government, the first Philopon addict was admitted into a Tokyo hospital one year after the signing ceremony in Tokyo Harbor. Hundreds of thousands would soon follow.

The Philopon problem became so grave so quickly that in 1948 a law was rushed through the Japanese parliament to regulate stimulants. The following year the Ministry of Health chose to prohibit the production of methamphetamine—but only in its tablet and powder form, a curious move that would prove a colossal blunder. The liquid form was left unregulated, and the country was promptly consumed by an epidemic of intravenous use, the most addictive and destructive application of the drug.

Not until the following year were all forms of methamphetamine prohibited in Japan, but the genie was out of the bottle. Pharmaceutical companies were as addicted to easy profits as users were to liquid methamphetamine. Several companies continued production, moving the liquid onto the black market, spawning a great flourish of domestic criminal syndicates. Records kept by the Japanese government show that by 1951 police confiscated an incredible 4.6 million vials of injectionable methamphetamine and arrested more than 17,000 people for using, manufacturing, or dealing the drug. Three years later, in 1954, the number had tripled to 55,000.

In the midst of the epidemic Japanese law enforcement began to note some trends unique to this particular drug, trends that would foretell what was to come decades later in distant lands. According to the National Research Institute of Police Science in Tokyo, Japanese police saw the epidemic moving from urban to rural areas. They also noted a dramatic increase in the importation of ephedrine, a precursor chemical and active ingredient vital to making methamphetamine. Perhaps most disturbing of all, police were coming across increasingly sophisticated clandestine labs in thousands of small Japanese towns. As a result, there was little evidence of smuggling connections with other countries. There was no need. All that was required to make enormous batches of meth could be purchased legally in general stores and drug stores scattered throughout the countryside.

For the time being the situation wasn't nearly so dire in the United States. But if you were trying to glimpse what was to come, you could see it. Amphetamine tablets or "pep pills," as they were coming to be known, began to replace caffeine tablets in truck stops and college campuses across the country where hundreds of thousands of veterans were taking classes on the G.I. Bill. And it was the Cold War, a phenomenon that captured events great and small in its orbit.

By 1949 millions of inhalers made by the Smith Kline and French Company were dismantled by recreational drug users to get at the amphetamine-soaked paper strips inside. The problem became so acute that the company was pressured into taking the inhalers off the market. This was particularly necessary as Congress had weighed-in on the recreational use of amphetamine and concluded that it was part of the "Red menace."

California Superior Court Judge Twain Michelsen was sure he was witnessing something that not only he but no one had ever seen before: hundreds of folks with horribly decayed teeth, skin lesions, and haggard gazes—all of whom were said to be hooked on drugs with names he'd never heard of. This was America's first generation of amphetamine addicts passing through his courtroom, a whole population that seemed completely alien to 1950s America. Testifying before a House subcommittee that was holding hearings on amphetamine abuse, Judge Michelsen attributed the growing epidemic to "Communist China's effort to despoil this country and other Western countries."

Although no direct and credible evidence was ever revealed to back up such a claim, the amphetamine problem was very real. But in the U.S. it was still more or less unique to coastal California, and Congress effectively dismissed it as a real threat to domestic harmony. Dr. Halsey Hurt, the U.S. assistant Surgeon General testified before the House Ways and Means Committee in 1955, saying that as far as he knew, amphetamine was "not addicting in the true sense of the word."

The Ranch

9

They were heady days. Not so long ago company stock was splitting with audacious regularity, making thousands of employees on-paper millionaires. My boss was said to be the richest man in the world. But everyone within my realm worked around the clock to make it happen, and we all, to a person, led exceedingly narrow lives. Summon the composite memory and it is a slur of unaccounted for days and nights spent before the chromatic glow of a monitor solving problems that seemed mere intellectual games, riddles to occupy the mind, a kind of cotton-candy entertainment. At times it seemed the ultimate absurdity that I should be paid for what seemed to amount to killing time.

But time only plays dead and is forever on the move. Turn your head, look up, look down, and your hair is thin and gray. Whenever this fact descended upon me, I was struck by another reality. It is impossible to feel truly alive working ninety hours every week encased in a glass building. Through some mysterious process fueled by low-grade but longstanding anxiety I came to associate misery with smallness (microcircuitry, for instance), and happiness with vastness, with wide-open spaces.

I found what I was looking for in the geographical center of Texas, a half-hour's drive from my parents' house. Walking the perimeter of hay fields and groves of hardwoods, I decided that a ranch was where I could accumulate experience apart from the virtual kind. Raw land. All it needed was habitation, and someone to look after it and some livestock while I was away.

My parents happily took up the task of finding a contractor to build a small house, and a ranch hand who could not only manage cattle but operate a bulldozer. With a small lake and a few scattered ponds, two-hundred head of cattle could easily live off the hay produced by irrigated fields. But the lake and ponds would first have to be carved out of the earth. Dad soon had the man with the résumé—a young local fellow who had run cattle on a large area ranch. He not only knew how to operate a D-6 Caterpillar but how to maintain the famously temperamental machine. He was, as Dad said, "a church-going man." Church-going had a dual meaning which was not lost on me: a Texan incapable of harboring impure thoughts like avarice. Only the owner's cattle would be allowed on the property, payment would reward work actually done. A church-going man's mind operated by the large, visible gears of simple virtue. Such a man's instincts demanded that he not take advantage of an owner who spent his workweek in Houston.

The first time I ever laid eyes on Clyde Pierson he was walking up the lane with my father, short-billed Nascar cap pulled down over his head, a forearm shielding his eyes from the leveling late-afternoon sun. He was carrying a feral hog trap, a metal cage used to snare indigenous swine that tear up pasture with their tusks in search of subterranean insect life.

Dad made the introductions, smiling down on us as we shook hands. Clyde had already put in his first week of work, Dad said. In that time he'd mended the north fence, cleared and burned a mountain of brush, set a dozen traps. Two of the creatures had been snared that morning. In spite of this one memory, I can recall no distinct first impression of Clyde himself. He was merely a redneck who was said to know what he was doing, and attended an evangelical church. Didn't talk much. I figured such a guy didn't have much to say.

Over the course of a month, which I'd taken off work to move into the new house, Clyde appeared to live up to his billing. We picked out a dozer and had it delivered. Work on the lake commenced. In that time I saw him driving to and from Sunday services at the Church of Christ just a couple miles down the road. Wednesday night was bible study, Thursday night he drove the kids to choir practice. Didn't have a lot in common, but mutual proximity and isolation meant we'd come to know each other well.

Clyde was proud of being from the small town of Franklin. He was also proud of never having been on an airplane, and claimed never to have wandered more than a hundred miles from his front porch. "Never left Texas," he liked to say.

But he had a past. One morning while the dozer idled he told me how he'd had a run-in with the law some time ago, before he was "saved." He lit a cigarette, pulled it from his mouth. "Spousal abuse," he grunted.

"So you were charged?"

"But never indicted," he said emphatically as he stared down at the coal of his cigarette, as though he were speaking to it. "I was drunk. Cops came out to the place and I fired a twelve-gauge into the air."

Later in the morning a guy from the satellite TV company came out to install a dish. He finished up just in time for lunch. I made Clyde and myself a sandwich, then began flipping through the channels until I came upon an episode of "South Park." Clyde put his sandwich down and groaned.

"Not a fan?" I asked.

"Show's the most sacrilegious thing I ever saw."

Out of deference to my employee's religious sensibilities I moved on to the CNBC for a stock market update.

"This is where your paycheck comes from," I murmured.

Clyde shrugged. Whatever.

That afternoon I got a call from the office. I had to be in New York City by noon the next day. Cursing under my breath, I packed a bag and headed out to tell Clyde. I could see the yellow dozer through the trees moving lugubriously back and forth, back and forth, back and forth. It took some yelling and then some waving to get his attention. He finally stopped the dozer and hurriedly but carefully extinguished his "cigarette" with a wetted thumb and forefinger. Then he killed the engine.

"That's not a cigarette, is it, Clyde?"

"A little something a cousin has growing on the back forty," he said as he hopped down, resigned to the fact that he had just lost his job.

"I don't want to see my Cat tumbling into the lake."

"I don't either, Mr. Braswell," he mumbled.

"Insurance companies don't see it as their responsibility to replace equipment destroyed by an operator who's high. Submit a $50,000 claim, they demand a drug test, and I'm stuck with a note on a dozer that doesn't run."

His head bobbed in agreement as he gazed down at the ragged tops of his sneakers.

"I'd be tempted myself," I said, now feeling a little sorry for this underpaid religious hypocrite. "I mean, I can't imagine the monotony you must live with…" Then, holding up a finger to mark a change in subject, I added, "Look, I've got to go to New York. I'll be back by the weekend."

Clyde suddenly lifted his gaze and pretended to be put out by this, as if I were indispensable to the operation. How was he going to get along without me? Then he pretended to give up and just let me take off on this silly junket.

"Give my regards to Broadway," he hollered cheerily as he climbed back on the Cat.

In New York I put out a small fire with a big client, and by the end of the week I was back in Houston, just as I'd planned. From there I drove up to the ranch to find Clyde in the kitchen in the midst of replacing the hood-vent over the stove. Looking up from his work, flathead screwdriver prying the sheet metal from the cabinetry, he appeared outraged.

"You owe me a hundred thirty-eight dollars and forty-four cents," he barked.

"What happened?"

"When you left last Monday you had the stovetop burners going full blast."

"What?"

"Nearly burned the place down. I came by a couple hours later for a drink, and the paint's curling off the metal...You're lucky you got me around, Mr. Braswell!"

Lucky, indeed. But after Clyde left curiosity seemed to sprout out of a bed of skepticism. I stepped up to the stove, turned on all four burners, and just let them go. The hood became warm, never hot.

But maybe conditions were different, perhaps something flammable on the stovetop. I couldn't say because I couldn't remember. *If only.* Soon gratitude overwhelmed uncertainty, and I found myself muttering, "Thank God for Clyde." If only I knew then of the trouble that lay in store. If only I could have grasped the significance of this imminently forgettable episode. But such is the nature of the gravest trouble: it so artfully poses as benevolence.

10

In the first two decades after World War II amphetamines were not only legal but relatively free of any meaningful social stigma. Benzedrine, Dexadrine, and Methedrine tablets were legally manufactured and widely distributed. These pep pills could be openly bought at student unions and truck stops, and few thought much about side—or long-term effects. This was mainstream America's little helper, the thing that got the 'burbs through the night.

American servicemen in Korea found amphetamines useful for the same reasons soldiers did in the previous war. Some, however, found a new recipe in substituting amphetamine for cocaine and mixing it with heroine to make the traditional speedball. This, of course, was not a military application but a purely recreational one, and one they brought home to America.

All the while Benzedrine had been gaining popularity in America's nascent counterculture, quickly becoming a favorite on both coasts. The pervasive use of Benzedrine among Beatnik society in particular has everything to do with the cultural phenomenon of drug use among young people, and the cognitive effect of psycho stimulants in general. Some well-publicized experimentation with amphetamine by a few underground celebrities lent an aura of authenticity, of real-life credentials, to their artistic personaes and work—a vital ingredient in a burgeoning youth culture. Put in contemporary idiom, speed was thought to have something to do with being "real" and thus on the cusp of becoming cool.

Amphetamine is unique among recreational drugs used in the fifties, as it left a lasting imprint on the work of the most influential artists of the day. This is most plainly evident in the folklore surrounding the actual writing of Jack Kerouac's seminal novel *On the Road*, published in 1957. Emblematic of all things Beat, Kerouac claimed he wrote the manuscript during a twenty-day creative spasm while on a Benzedrine high. The telling detail lies in his account of writing the book on a massive spool of telegraph paper that fed into the typewriter carriage, enabling him to work continually without having to reload every time he came to the bottom of a page. For those twenty days he slept only in brief fits, experimenting with a literary technique he would call "spontaneous prose," a literary incarnation of the jazz improvisation Kerouac discovered in the jazz bars of San Francisco and became so fond of.

The essence of this spontaneous prose is the act of putting down on paper whatever comes to mind, chronicling "the noise of the mind" unedited. It is an approach to the literary arts that bespeaks the very nature of amphetamine on the disposition of cognitive processes, as the drug both demands and develops single-mindedness, predisposing the user to become either vacantly unaware or perhaps violently intolerant of minor distractions. Unfortunately spontaneous prose wasn't as artistically successful as its jazz counterpart. As Truman Capote famously quipped about Kerouac's famous twenty-day literary spree: "That isn't writing, that's *type*-writing."

Through the years Kerouac and his unbuttoned literary style became representative of the entire Beat counterculture in which adherence to form was replaced by a commandment of free expression. Over time Kerouac became addicted to Benzedrine, finally developing thrombophlebitis, a form of heart disease common to amphetamine users. But the impact of Kerouac's work and that of his literary compatriots would be lasting. By the time the sixties rolled around, free-form artistic expression reflecting a free-form lifestyle would become the hallmark of the far more broadly based hippie movement in America.

11

By the autumn of 1998 it becomes our habit on the weekends to drive up to the ranch from Houston to escape the city. Lucille has taken to the routine. Early each morning Emily and I head out into the half-light to feed the cattle, mend fence, scatter fish food across the pond surface. Through the course of the morning she rides in my lap on the tractor, upon my shoulders as we walk along the shore of the pond, on the gas tank of the four-wheeler. Her blond hair, light as cornsilk, blows in the wind. Eventually Clyde arrives, waving from his truck as it wobbles over the double-track road toward the dozer. Once he commences his work the peacefulness of the morning is obliterated.

All the while Lucille lies in bed, face down, lost in a long interval of sleep that has interrupted an even longer interval of wakefulness. For the last few weeks now she takes work shifts two-and three-at-a-time, then abandons herself to a full night and a sunny day entombed in a pile of bedding. Next morning she might spend at home organizing the garage, working through the night till the place is as neat as a bandbox. But for now she sleeps.

The sun lofts over the trees just as the chores are completed. Emily and I head to the concrete cattle trough near the gate to the ranch. The day has warmed, so we strip down to our underwear and splash about, and then walk to the pond where we fish. Not until early afternoon does Lucille appear, arms tightly crossed about her ribs, eyes swollen as though from bee stings. She slowly absorbs the scene, and then smiles and shakes her head. The picture as a whole is lovely, but a little too country for her.

Later that morning we head to town to a mall with a daycare center where we can leave Emily while Lucille and I shop. We move from store to store as she collects dresses, jewelry and shoes along the way. Eventually we come to a lingerie store where she wants to try on some underthings. She leads me along from rack to rack, holding up a pair of panties, a silk bra. I smile. She smiles. She then takes my hand and leads me into a dressing room where she begins to exhibit some of the behavior that, in my experience with women, is unique to her.

That we are in a public place seems to incite Lucille's carnal nature. This time, for my sole pleasure, she wants complete strangers to imagine what's going on behind the slat door. But this peep show has an alternate purpose.

"Think I look fat?" she asks, running her hands over her tummy.

"Not at all."

"I'm going to burn off a few pounds."

"But you're not overweight."

"What about my breasts? Too small?"

"I love your breasts," I whisper as a woman asks a sales girl two feet away if the store carries Wonderbra.

Lucille cups each hemisphere with either hand.

"They shrank after Emily," she says with an air of unabashed frankness. "There's a clinic back in Houston…they've done thousands of women. Five-thousand dollars."

I sense that I'm shaking my head.

"I've been working two extra shifts each week," she says. "I want to spend the money on you."

"___"

In time the straps of the sundress are dragged over her shoulders, the dress buttoned up. We gather up Lucille's boxes and bags, and head down to a Benni-gans for a drink. As the sound system pipes old hits from the eighties throughout the restaurant, Lucille mumbles, "I want to look beautiful for you."

"You already do," I say abruptly, and the conversation ends right there.

After a couple of whiskey and sodas, we pick up Emily and head back home. By the time we arrive she's asleep. We put her down for the night, and then Luci-lle and I settle in for the evening on the sofa. Lucille scans the pay-per-view chan-nels and finally settles on a movie with a title like "Sticky Fingers" or "Nasty Fingers"—something sexy and stupid, old fashioned soft-core. As we watch, she curls herself into me like a cat, her feline back molding itself to my lap, her hand stroking my chest. Then Lucille makes it clear she's in the mood for the real thing, in the midst of which she whimpers, "I want to look beautiful for you."

And she is instantly worked into a lather. Once the moment is complete, she nuzzles her nose into my neck, and calmly says, "A lot of women are having theirs done—a lot of your friends' wives." And she begins ticking off names.

"You really need to think about why you want to do this."

With that she kisses my neck. Before long, she's in my lap, and this time there's a relentless ardor in the cadence of her movements. Smothering my head in her arms, her skull rolling against mine, she murmurs something. When I ask her what she said, she murmurs again, "I need you."

Time stops. Lucille's dark hair pours over my head and for a moment it is as though we are behind a waterfall, the rest of the world closed out. And for that

one moment a single thought eclipses all lingering doubt about the innate good-
ness of our relationship, about the necessity of it. Lucille needs me. As I drift off
to sleep that night, I realize that I am in love for the first time in this everyday life
of mine.

◆   ◆   ◆

Once or twice a week Dad climbs into his truck and makes the fifteen-minute
drive out to the ranch to check on the property, to see that the house is still standing, that the cattle are fenced in and not wandering about central Texas. But he
really comes out to collect deer antlers, tramp the woods, get away from the buzz
and drone of civilization. At sixty-eight he goes everywhere with a pair of binoculars swinging about his neck, making mental notes of the species of birds, the
number of white-tail deer and feral hogs. Then one day as he looks through the
binoculars he thinks he sees what looks like a spot of trash beneath a distant
locust tree, the trunk of which is swarming with raspberry nettles.

He makes through the tall grass and sees at once that this is not trash at
all—that is, everything has been carefully and deliberately stored here. From this
nest of alfalfa and raspberry branches he pulls out a large plastic zip-lock freezer
bag holding a brick of driveway cleaner. The others contain engine starter fluid,
stick matches, D-cell batteries, light bulbs. Empty Coleman propane canisters are
clustered on the bottom like dinosaur eggs. What's all this garage clutter doing
way out here, anyway? Lifting the final bag, he sees it is filled with hypodermic
needles.

Within the hour it is on its way to a landfill, the first leg of its journey on its
way to being forgotten.

The Kids are All Right

12

Stories surrounding drug use among American servicemen during the Vietnam War have long ago ascended into ether of myth. Hollywood found it dramatic theatre. Francis Ford Coppola's "Apocalypse Now" captures the hallucinogenic madness of that time and place, but in the process exaggerates wildly the currency of hallucinogenics themselves.

By far the most prevalent illicit drug used by American fighting men in Vietnam was marijuana. The reason was largely economic, as ten dollars bought a half-pound of pot, and a can of legal but warm beer, by comparison, cost fifty cents. The most tension relief for the G.I.'s buck came in a very large "feedbag."

The reality that seems to have evaporated in the mists of time is that almost no American soldiers ever smoked pot prior to or during a potential combat situations. To stay alive and to keep one's comrades alive, one had to remain alert. Vietnam vets are of one mind on the subject: compromising awareness would be reckless in the extreme and simply not tolerated. Go pills, or amphetamines, on the other hand, were seen for what they could do for the platoon or squadron. By keeping everyone alert they kept everyone alive.

A clear picture as to the kinds of amphetamines made available and to what extent they were used is difficult to come by, as official documentation is almost nonexistent. The best that can be discerned is by way of anecdotal evidence and the few disclosures that have been made by the military. The government's apprehension in providing data on amphetamine use is due, presumably, to the perceived contradiction in clamping down on drugs in civilian life while dispensing them among the military ranks abroad. This perceived inconsistency, however, doesn't necessarily make the military application illegitimate or the government's position hypocritical. On the contrary, amphetamines have proven their worth by dramatically reducing the rate of mishap in situations where fatigue degrades mental acuity. The military, after all, routinely finds itself in extraordinary circumstances, and statistics clearly show they saved the lives of military personnel. Though a few facts have survived, an informational brown-out was imposed.

Not until the dawn of the war in Vietnam did the Pentagon officially sanction the use of amphetamines by servicemen. The decision was likely made based on government tests conducted in the late 1940s and early 1950s that indicated amphetamine use typically improved mental performance in pilots by approximately five percent—often the difference between safely landing on a carrier deck in heavy seas at night and colliding with it. The Air Force was the first to make the drug available to pilots and aircrew, seeing a potential benefit in extended flight operations. Strategic Air Command (SAC) approved limited use of amphetamines in 1960, and Tactical Air Command (TAC) in 1962. They would keep using it for decades to come, as modern flight operations require around-the-clock air support. Tactical air craft can be flown in all weather conditions, day or night, for prolonged periods with the support of air tankers.

During the Vietnam War amphetamines were soon made generally available in tablet form to all branches of the armed services. But their niche was with the Air Force, Army pilots, and among servicemen pulling guard duty in perimeter defense positions. In the latter case amphetamines in the form of Obestol, which was produced by a French pharmaceutical company, was used to counter fatigue and the crush of sheer boredom endemic to the task. Veterans reported side-effects that included a feeling of being wired, loss of appetite, and general nervousness. As a countermeasure, Binoctol, a barbiturate, was made available in ten and twenty-five milligram strengths. To a very limited degree, this allowed servicemen to grab a kind of sleep, edgy and fitful as it might be. As the war deepened with no end in sight, amphetamines were made as available as cigarettes to any serviceman who thought he might need them.[1]

Presiding over the initial phases of the conflict of course was President Kennedy, who suffered from Addison's disease and severe chronic back pain. To treat the ailments and to boost his energy level, his personal physician, Dr. Max Jacobson, the original "Dr. Feelgood" and something of a doctor-to-the-stars, gave the president injections of an amphetamine cocktail three times daily, along with a steroid regime—a combination that could easily lead to manic behavior. The result of the amphetamine injections alone, it is widely believed, only enhanced Kennedy's legendary sexual appetite. The president's brother, Bobby, insisted on having Jacobson's concoctions tested by the Food and Drug Administration. JFK's response was pragmatic and colorful: "I don't care if it's horse piss. It works."

According to Seymour Hersh, in his book on the Kennedy Administration, *The Dark Side of Camelot* (Little Brown and Company, 1997), the president's allegedly voracious sexual cravings included threesomes with Hollywood starlets

---

1.   "Stimulant Use in Extended Flight Operations," Lt. Col. Rhonda Cornum, U.S. Army, Dr. John Caldwell, Lt. Col. Kory Cornum, U.S. Air Force.

and all-night pool parties with European socialites and prostitutes. President Kennedy is also said to have told a friend of the family that if he didn't get "a strange piece of ass" every day he would come down with a migraine headache. In composite his reckless behavior and heightened sexual appetite appear to be classic manifestations of a man receiving regular amphetamine injections.

Some had more apocalyptic concerns with the president's amphetamine use. In 1972 a *New York Times* reporter quoted one of President Kennedy's physicians as having warned the president that he was putting the free world at risk, writing in a letter, "...no President with his finger on the red button has any business taking stuff like that." In 1975, long after it was learned what he had prescribed the president, Dr. Max Jacobson was stripped of his medical license.

Ironically it was President Kennedy's administration that sought legislation requiring new drug testing procedures for amphetamines, along with warning labels and tighter controls. In effect, JFK wrought this control over drugs he himself was taking for questionable reasons. But the need for regulation was clear and present in the country. Federal officials estimated that in the early 1960s approximately eight billion legally manufactured amphetamine and barbiturate tablets were in circulation domestically. The culprit was the medical profession in general. As Dr. Lester Grinspoon, a professor of psychiatry at Harvard Medical School noted, "Just a couple of decades ago, this was being prescribed by the ton-load...physicians really believed it was like a panacea and that there was no downside." The American Medical Association, along with the pharmaceutical industry, lobbied congress with the message that additional legislation wasn't warranted.

Meanwhile the drug took root in an unlikely corner of America. Indeed, the President of the United States and American fighting forces in Vietnam had something in common with, of all people, American housewives—a segment of the population quickly developing a curious weakness for the drug. The stereotype emphasizes the plump, joy-deprived housewife watching soap operas and munching snacks while her distracted husband languished at the office. These women were not after the same heightened state of alertness as their sons in the rice patties and jungles of Southeast Asia. For them—as a group—the draw lay in the enhanced self-confidence the drug provides along with its unique ability to suppress the appetite. The latter trait perhaps fed the first when one spent the balance of the day within a few footsteps of a stocked refrigerator. In any event, the Drug Abuse Control Amendment of 1962 referred to amphetamines, along with barbiturates and LSD, as dangerous, and allowed the FDA control over them.

The Haight-Ashbury District of San Francisco would be the fertile ground from which the amphetamine problem would bloom and spread throughout the United States. In the 1960s doctors in the Bay area began prescribing amphetamine injections for treatment of a variety of ailments that included heroine addiction. Soon local pharmacies began selling injectable amphetamines without prescriptions, or with forged prescriptions, many of which were quite amateurishly scrawled. Sometimes they would take phony telephone orders from users posing as doctors, other times the physicians actually had medical licenses. These were some of the earliest "scriptwriters"—physicians who, for the price of an office visit, would write prescriptions for pharmaceutical drugs. Soon the whole charade got entirely out of hand. By 1967 the craze hit its peak with 31 million such prescriptions being written for amphetamine nationwide (of course most of these were only for the tablet form of the drug, which were incredibly cheap, with a thousand tablets costing less than a dollar well into the sixties). A disproportionate amount of the practice of amphetamine injection was limited to the Haight. Little did anyone suspect that this was mere prelude to a truly horrifying show.

Britain was seeing something of the very same phenomenon concerning amphetamine tablets. There, as in America, prescriptions could be easily got from the family doctor. According to Rowdy Yates, former heroin addict and current author and senior lecturer on addiction studies at the University of Stirling in Scotland, "There were less formal means of acquisition, with pills available in clubs and East London cafes where they could even be ordered in one's coffee." U.S. Air Force personnel were known to sell Benzedrine tablets they'd taken from their cockpit emergency kits. Sometimes they sold the drugs to Londoners, or stay up all night dancing in the clubs after popping the Bennies themselves.

Amphetamine abuse in Britain became a problem so quickly that the issue was raised in parliament, and in 1964 the Prevention of Misuse Act was passed. By then, however, Black Bombers, Dexies, and Purple Hearts were as popular as the Beatles. With the withdrawal of the over-the-counter status and newfound caution among physicians who wrote prescriptions, the illicit trade was born. England suddenly had a problem on its hands: a great many jittery mothers were now walking the back streets of bad neighborhoods looking for what their family health care providers and pharmacists had once provided. And so were their children, many of whom liked to call themselves "Mods."

A contraction of "Modernists," the Mods were a new incarnation among a dizzying array of emerging British youth cultures. As a group they were distinctly urban, and shared a taste for sharp clothes, dance clubs, Italian scooters, and their mothers' amphetamines. The males among them also seemed distinctly disinterested in women. University education lay squarely in their future, and when it came test time, they knew how to make themselves alert. They would become a precursor to the Northern Soul movement in Britain, and ultimately the rave scene in both America and England thirty years later. Yates, who has studied the phenomenon closely, characterizes all three as "incarnations of modern-day dandies."

One of the most enduring aspects of Mod culture was one of its defining aspects: the Mods' image as dabblers. And their drug of choice for this working—and middle-class youth culture was Drinamyl, a powerful amphetamine. Mods tended to be low-born smart kids educated in public schools who aspired to join the ranks of the patricians whose parents ran the world. Wired on Drinamyl, they made a habit of dancing through the night at up-scale West End clubs such as The Scene, the Crazy Elephant, and The Flamingo, none of which, significantly, sold alcohol. The Mods' amphetamine-friendly predecessors, the American Beats, were a decidedly not-cricket bunch who happily staked their claim to the margins of society. The Mods by contrast saw themselves *as* society, wizened upwardly-mobile children of accountants who wanted to feel as at home on the streets of Mayfair as they did in East End alleyways. Where the Beatniks concerned themselves with the arts, the Mods were drawn more along the lines of fashion mavens. Like their hair, their collars were short, ties thin, mo-hair suits trim—all in all more corporate yuppy than artsy bohemian. In his seminal book, *If it Weren't for the Alligators: A History of Drugs, Music and Popular culture in Manchester*, Yates makes a concise observation: "To working class kids it [Mod culture] was a dream lying just outside the factory gate. To them—unable to play music, paint murals, write poetry—the one sure way in was to take the same drugs."

Mod music is epitomized by early Who albums, whose lead singer, Roger Daltry, stammered the lyrics "I hope I die before I get old." The stammer, it was understood in privy quarters, was the result of a mild amphetamine overdose. The Mod scene was documented in the film "Quadrophenia," which captured this curiously British phenomenon of skinny young men on scooters zipping off to coastal towns such as Brighton and Hastings to rumble with "Rockers," another British youth culture movement whose sympathies lay with traditional rock and roll over modern rock, a pure fifties image over the sixties, Buddy Holly over Jamaican ska, motorcycles over scooters, beer over Purple Hearts.

Looking back at the scene through the prism of nearly forty years, it all appears superfluously idiotic or, at best, eccentric. But it surely meant a great deal to the young people whose late adolescent identity was all about being a Mod or a Rocker, or what have you. The Mod scene was of somewhat lasting significance if only for one impression it made on later incarnations of youth culture. And it is this: to be a Mod was to think of oneself as modern, and to be modern meant to be not only smart but hyper-alert. Surely it could be said that these are the salient qualities of every the modern man and woman alive today, the very ethos of Starbucks, of corporate coffeehouse culture.

13

Lucille lies on her side, fast asleep, the crown of her forehead misshapen, the line of the left eye swooping in a great bulbous arc up into the forehead. I pull her over to me, and then I see the skin parted above the temple, just below the hairline, a crescent about three-quarters of an inch long. Blood has saturated and dried within the cotton pillow case, stiffening it like a great tortilla. In a panic I try to awaken her by slapping her bottom. She comes-to very slowly.

Annoyed rather than startled, she says, "What's wrong?"

"Baby, your head is bleeding!"

I pull her to her feet and lead her into the bathroom before the mirror.

She studies the raised plum-purple oval encasing the split seam of the wound, fingertips lightly surveying the crevasse.

"Must have hit my head last night…"

"You don't remember doing it?"

Her right eye blinks while her left only flinches like a tiny fist. She shakes her head. After cleaning herself with the corner of a bath towel it's back to bed where she falls instantly to sleep.

Late in the morning, her eye gruesomely swollen over a mug of hot coffee, Lucille says she has to leave for Austin today. She's scheduled for a routine interview at the state medical board to review her work at Weiss Clinic. The interview happens to be at a hospital, so she'll have her forehead stitched up in the emergency room beforehand. I remind her that it's her birthday. She smiles and nods.

"So happy birthday."

She accepts an exceedingly gentle kiss on the cheek, and we go our separate ways.

The rest of my day is all about work, after which I come home to find Lucille curled up on the sofa, a pink butterfly-bandage stretched across her forehead. Seven stitches. The interview went well, she says, as did the sewing up. Then she lapses into a melancholy quiet and seems to get mired there. To perk her spirits, I take her out to a birthday dinner at a steakhouse where she sits across from me, not saying much. When I ask if anything's wrong, she shakes her head. In the silence I remind myself that marriage is about good times and bad, that it is her birthday and the moment has arrived. So I reach for my pocket. "You once told me your birthday would be marked by significant events," I say.

Her good eye ogles the tiny black velvet box as I withdraw my hand. She pries it open, and her gloom seems to lift like fog.

"It comes with a house," I add. "One with lots of room for Emily."

With the question comes the answer, and then a murmured, "It's *beautiful*," repeated again and again.

So it's done. I'm thinking, I have asked this woman to marry me and she is now wearing my ring. In the moment I try to contemplate all that this means. Lost as I am in this convection of thought, I nevertheless notice Lucille lapsing back into her former melancholy. Then it occurs to me. She's about to twist the ring from her hand and press it back into its soft case. Tears and a garbled apology are at hand. I let a little silence fall before asking what's wrong. She won't say.

"I just asked for your hand in marriage," I say as tears crest over her cheeks. "What's going on?"

"I don't deserve this," she whimpers. "You really don't know...who I am..."

I cradle her chin between my forefinger and thumb.

"Stop right there," I say.

She breaks into a smile, and the mood slowly drifts away like weather.

The following weekend I am on my way to the ranch where Lucille will be meeting me later tonight. Talkradio voices pulse through the airwaves over the noise of rushing wind. A quick stop at a liquor store in a redneck town for a Coke, and I'm again on my way.

The sun is descending into the woods when I arrive, the gate open. My parents are here for the weekend, the yellow flames of their barbecue glimmer through the forest. I park the car at the house and head down to the fire under the walnut tree beside the pond. Heart-felt greetings and congratulations on the engagement, and I fix myself a drink. Hotdogs hang impaled at the end of sharpened sticks over a bed of good hardwood coals. Dad tells me about the weird collection of trash he came across, "only it was stashed so neatly...couldn't make heads nor tails of it..." But I am too happy, tired and distracted by my workaday world for a mystery, so after a little dinner I climb on a four-wheeler and chase hogs through the dusky light. After a few minutes of this I'm finally ready to relax, to await the arrival of my wife-to-be with my parents around the fire. When I pull up, my mother approaches in the radiant light. But her expression shows something unexpected as she comes into full view. She's concerned, even worried.

"Dustin called a moment ago," she says, holding a cell phone. "He wanted you to call him back right away."

I take the phone to the car where I can plug it into the cigarette lighter to get better service out here in the sticks. But when he answers there is no familiar small talk, no customary bullshitting.

Point-blank, he asks, "Do you know what Stadol is?"

I ask him why he wants to know.

He pauses.

"I've received a report."

"A report? What are you—a federal agent?"

He pauses again, and nimbly adjusts his tone to that of a concerned friend.

"Sterling, over a hundred prescriptions were written for it by Lucille."

"Yeah?"

"A third of them were written in your name."

He then delineates Stadol's medical and addictive properties: snorted through the nose in vapor form by way of an inhaler; the high is an intense trip to the moon with few visible side-effects, hence its popularity among medical professionals.

"They were all written within a three-month period," Dustin adds. "She's been snorting Stadol like fresh air."

A long silence filled by cell phone static.

"There's one more thing…the head of the department has gotten ahold of the report. He's required to turn this kind of information over to the police."

"Have you told Lucille?"

"We had a talk a few days ago."

"Last Tuesday?"

"If I remember right."

"I proposed to her that night."

Dustin is silent for a long while.

"She probably needs professional help," he finally says. "Sorry to be the one to tell you, bud."

After hanging up I wander through the evening light to where the fire has collapsed into a shallow mound of coals, the orange bed reflecting on the surface of the pond like a setting sun. I stand alongside my mother, absently staring deep into the phosphorescence. She notices my quiet mood and allows me dwell. My father rakes the coals with the butt of a walnut stick.

A few minutes later a pair of headlights swings through the darkness. My parents and I head toward the house where Lucille's car is parked. A hug and a kiss, and then I gently lift Emily out of back seat. The dog sniffs at my crotch, the cat curls tightly around my ankle in a motion of amorous recognition. I bring the little girl into the foyer, and there we pause under the chandelier, bathed in light before my mother and father who are smiling upon us. This is their domesticated son. This is their boy, about to become a family man after all these years.

That night Lucille and I are curled up on the sofa watching Letterman. Out of the clear blue, without consciously rehearsing what I'm about to say, I tell her I know why she hit her head.

She sits up but doesn't turn to me. Then she says with a clear challenge ringing in her voice, "So why did I hit my head?"

I tell her.

Without a word she then rises from the sofa and heads off to the bedroom. The door closes, the tumblers rotate and lock.

Sometime long after midnight I awake on the sofa. Dread descends through the darkness. Its source is the fear that my fiancée's head is haunted.

14

It would become the next generation of what could now be called amphetamine youth culture. This time around it arrived in the form of a musical revival movement that found expression on the sprung wooden floors of basement clubs of northwest England. Though little known in America, the musical component of the Northern Soul movement of the sixties and seventies was lifted from 1950s Motown and temporally and geographically transplanted to the British working-class towns of northern England.

Made up of aficionados of dated Motown rarities pressed in vinyl, this peculiar child of the Mod scene would, on the surface, seem antithetical to the sentimental and backward-looking Northern Soul crowd. Disciples spent hours pouring through warehoused crates of never-released Motown forty-fives in search of a specific sound they intuitively and collectively recognized as pure. What they had in common with the Mods was conceptual—an appreciation of an extremely specific brand of music and pill culture. Again, amphetamines were the drug of choice, as they enhanced the dance and music. One of amphetamine's hallmark characteristics, of course, is its ability to propel the body in compulsive, repetitive motion.

But the Northern Soul movement consisted of a very different class of Englishmen. According to Rowdy Yates, Northern Soul, as a group, would have thought the idea of scooters as stupid. "As far as they were concerned, scooters were what middle class grammar school boys rode around London on. People into Northern Soul were more like garage mechanics. It was the working class remnant of Mod culture, if you like."

To Yates their choice of amphetamine is also significant. "If you're working in a garage under a railway from eight till eight, weekends become important. It's the time you do your courting, it's the time you do your dancing, and let off steam. And if you wanted a drug to get you going on these three routes, you wouldn't look for an introspective drug like cannabis or LSD."

Dave Grodin, the man who gave the Northern Soul movement its name, was one of the central figures in establishing the British arm of Motown. In the late sixties he noted that Northerners preferred soul to its cousin, funk, the latter of which was popular in the south. The spirit of the movement was more than mere amphetamine-laced nostalgia. Northern Soul D.J.s became regional celebrities, and clubs like The Twisted Wheel, the Wigan Casino, and The Blackpool Mecca landmarks. At its height the Wigan Casino was said to have had 100,000 members. Of the tunes to have been resurrected were "Born a Loser" by Ron Day, "Here I Go Again," by Archie Bell and the Drells, and "All For You" by Earl Van Dyke—all of which were rediscovered after exhaustive culling. In many cases the tunes were recorded years, if not decades, before they became renowned in this unforeseeable movement of the Old World. By this circuitous route a great many of the songs would find their way to the top of the singles chart in England.

But the movement became troubled. A number of the clubs eventually fell upon hard times as widespread use of Methedrine spurred crime endemic to amphetamine abuse for both the patrons and owners alike. Some of the owners found ways around restrictions by hosting "all-dayers," as opposed to all-nighters. Diurnal or nocturnal, law enforcement authorities recognized them as the same amphetamine-driven dance sessions.

Northern soul's legacy is chiefly that of a remarkably vibrant musical revival of undiscovered artists. But it has an ancillary legacy as the precursor to the rave scene—the all-night, seemingly spontaneous dance parties in warehouse districts in England and America that would come a generation later. "Ravers," however, didn't inherit the beautifully esoteric musical tastes of the Northern Soul movement, but rather tediously throbbing techno-pop. What the rave scene did inherit was amphetamine in the form of methylenedioxymethamphetamine, or, as some call it, MDMA. What many of the millions who take the drug don't know is that the MA in this abbreviation represents methamphetamine. MDMA, of course, is more commonly known as Ecstasy.

In the U.S. during the late sixties amphetamines were undergoing a transformation that nearly extinguished it as a popular idea: among the burgeoning hippie movement sweeping the country it was thought to be a mom and dad drug. Amphetamines, and pills in general, ran counter to the mellowed-out philosophy common to pot-smoking vagabonds and LSD users who dropped out of school to follow their bliss. In the hazy dominions of the hippies, vapid sedation reigned supreme over teeth gnashing; edginess in any form was decidedly unhip. People with amphetamine jitters do not follow swamis; amphetamine was a thoroughly bourgeois drug taken by people who wanted to get something done—law students and housewives, and perhaps some of the proletariat such as truck drivers and shift workers. Of course not everyone in San Francisco with long hair was a hippie at heart, many of whom thought nothing could be more pleasant than injecting tremendous amounts of liquid amphetamine.

The idea of amphetamine was also still alive, if not thriving, in an unlikely nook of mainstream America. The cork lined music studios of Nashville saw country greats recording through consecutive days and nights. Some developed habits. Johnny Cash was arrested in El Paso, Texas for attempting to smuggle an acoustic guitar packed with prescription amphetamine into the country from Mexico. He later explained how he initially got hooked on the drug while hanging out with the truckers who drove musicians and all their gear to the Grand Ole Opry. Before he was done with amphetamines he would be hallucinating regularly and his health wrecked.

Cash's contemporary, Elvis Presley, found a darker fate, as he alternated between amphetamines and barbiturates prescribed to him by his personal physician to help him with his chronic nightmares and insomnia. While in the army he began stockpiling pills, and later found amphetamines helpful in dealing with a brutal performance and filming schedule. Between 1973 and 1977 he entered into serious drug withdrawal treatments at Baptist Hospital in Memphis, and a make-shift clinic was actually installed in his suite at the Las Vegas Hilton Hotel in order to keep his addiction out of the press. Much of the while, however, he was near death. Finally, in May of 1978, he suffered a heart attack at his Graceland estate, bloated and irrevocably caught up in the duality of a ruthless pharmacology.

Of course some are blessed in all endeavors and mysteriously made immortal. Hugh Hefner, the founder of Playboy Magazine, coasted through this contentious time in his pajamas surrounded by beautiful women, sustained by Pepsi, candy bars, and substantial doses of Dexadrine, a particularly potent form of amphetamine. In the eighties he suffered a stroke, but recovered, never to touch amphetamines again.

The significance of Hugh Hefner's, Johnny Cash's and Elvis Presley's use and abuse of amphetamine lay in their place in the social spectrum of their times. During the civil chaos of the sixties and seventies these personalities were decidedly mainstream whereas hippies were not. The elder generation preferred the formality of a prescription (if they could be had) or at least pharmaceuticals, while the younger counterculture went with freelancers who grew their own drugs wherever they could find suitably obscure acreage. But amphetamine culture was about to undergo a critical transformation with respect to how it was come by. Now that it was generally illegal and rigidly controlled as a prescribed medication, the adamant user and addict would have to forego the reassuring formality of a physician's approval or a pharmaceutical company's expertise.

15

The topic of engagement is broached. A final scene appeals to my imagination, somehow reminds me of a dust-devil coursing through the Hill Country. In the wake of the final exchange, there's a meaninglessness about the mess left behind.

"Safe and legal," is all I have to say.

She heads for the door, silently enraged that I can reduce the death of our love to three words of sarcasm. The door is opened. "Didn't think you'd ever give up on me, baby," she says.

"Do you even *know* you have a problem?"

She merely shakes her head, thoroughly crushed. I have failed her in the most fundamental way. The front door closes, and Lucille is gone. Once again.

When all of my curses have been shouted, all the dishes thrown like Frisbees across the dining room, lamps pushed over—everything is just as it was before. I am left in an empty and silent house among all my scattered things. The last few months might as well have been a dream. All around me lay the physical evidence of its turbulence.

The days pass just as they had before Lucille came back last May, a lifeless routine of work and sleep. When sad, I drink; when brokenhearted, I drink a lot. And so I undertake the latter course with gusto, leaving the world around me to fend for itself. Then a knock on the door one night pierces the vacuum. Standing in the doorway is Lucille's mother. The first words out of her unsmiling mouth are, "You and Lucille have too much between you. You can't just throw it all away."

She doesn't come inside, won't say another word. She merely turns on her heel and struts back to where her Impala is parked on the street.

Maybe she has a point with her two sentences. The life I began with her daughter has indeed taken on a momentum of its own. So the girl I love is a junkie: I am a lush. I'm still buying a house whether I want to or not. Earnest money has been put down, and earnest money will be paid.

While considering all of this the following evening in my quiet antique house, there's another knock at the door. I could be flashing back to high school, for again it's Lucille's mother, this time with Lucille.

"You two need to talk this out," her mother says.

Lucille stands at her side, a hand holding her elbows, eyes at my feet. Then, as before, her mother abruptly leaves, effectively stranding her daughter at my house. Moths gather about the porch light in her absence. Eventually Lucille levels her gaze, and then she comes into my arms.

But life is rarely so tidy as all this.

Before I can buy the house I have to collect a down payment of $100,000 from my account in Los Angeles. The simplest way to go about doing this is to physically go there and get it, as banks prefer to make large transactions the old fashioned way, in person. But a few weeks later, just as I'm putting a few things together in my bedroom—laying out some clothes, getting my financial papers together—I receive a call from Lucille's mother. She's stricken with panic. Lucille, she sputters in her raspy voice, has been arrested.

"Arrested for what?"

"Per, per, per—"

"Prescriptions? Lucille's been arrested for writing prescriptions?"

Lucille's mother grunts an affirmative, then "Kro...Kro...Kro..."

"She was arrested at a Kroger? Where is she now?"

Then in an exhalation, she breathes, "Sterling, *they took her to jail!*"

So the report has made its inevitable rounds, and Lucille has done what she was inevitably going to do. The result was foreordained.

Nevertheless, my flight leaves in an hour. If I'm not on that plane we won't be buying the house and will lose five-thousand dollars. So I am coolly trying to stay focused on the larger picture here. Lucille, I am thinking, is going to have to spend some time—perhaps the night—with a few of our local lady rummies and felons in a hot and crowded place. Perhaps an unpleasant episode will get her attention. Perhaps that would make the problem real to her.

With these thought in mind I hang up and put a call in to the Montgomery County Jail, and within a few minutes I have Lucille on the line. She's calm, but I can tell by her clotted voice that she's been crying. Then she says, "You need to come down here right away with the checkbook."

I imagine her standing in the shadowy corner of a basement jail holding a battered pay phone to her ear, a pink butterfly bandage spanning the purple seam of her healing head wound, a physical reminder of how she came to be here.

"You had to know you were going to get caught," I say.

"I just needed a Xanex," she chortles.

"I hope you still have some because you have put me in one hell of a predicament."

"Just come pick me up."

"You're going to have to spend the night where you are."

The connection is silent for a very long time.

"And now I have to get off the phone," I add.

With that she hangs up. I throw whatever I have on the bed into a bag, and it's out to the car and off to the airport. Upon approaching the United counter I am whisked off to the gate and onto the plane. A flight attendant of Scandinavian descent floats down the aisle with a sweat-beaded bottle of champagne and asks if I'd care for any…Ten minutes later the pilot announces that we're at 35,000 feet and heading for Los Angeles at eighty-five percent of speed of sound. The moment my champagne glass is voided, the attendant reappears to refill it.

"So you're heading to L.A.," she says. "Business or pleasure?"

I think about this for a long moment.

"It was supposed to be all business," I confide in this beautiful stranger. "See, I'm going to get some money for the down-payment on a house…but my fiancée's in jail back in Houston."

She laughs. I'm a real card. A fella with a sense of humor and a vivid imagination.

"Say, you wouldn't have any vodka?" I ask.

The introduction of spirits distorts space and time, lending the day a much needed sense of unreality. What seems but a moment later, we're descending into LAX and I find myself in a cab heading for a hotel. That night I sit up in bed watching movies. A whole host of attendants ferries up sandwiches, vodka, and soda water while I let my mind wander through a half-dozen movie plots. Early in the night the tug of responsibility becomes too much and I call Lucille's mother for some ballast, a link to abandoned reality. Lucille, she says, will be out tomorrow evening, courtesy of Mom and Dad. Then she adds, "Why didn't you bail her out?"

"I thought it important to gain her attention."

Voices more or less overlapping, they say, "Got her attention? What for?"

In very measured detail, I explain—in essence saying, We don't want our Lucille developing a problem, Gotta nip things in the bud, Tough love, Blah, blah, blah.

The rest of the conversation is a series of long cool silences.

The business of getting the money from the bank in the form of cashiers checks is simple enough, and by ten the following morning I have what I came for. My return flight to Houston leaves in two hours, but as I climb back in the cab for the hotel I realize I don't want to return. I call Dustin and talk for an hour or two about this new hyper-life of mine. All Dustin can say is, "Do not marry her, man. Not until she's been through rehab."

Immediately upon arrival I drive from the airport to Lucille's apartment where I find her on the living room floor playing with Emily. Her eyes are shot red from crying, although she isn't crying now. Not exactly serene, but more or less fine. She knows why I didn't bail her out, understands. She wouldn't have bailed herself out. Finally the topic of wedding plans comes up, and I buck myself up to tell her, "We've got too much going on with buying the house, these new legal matters…"

Then comes a torrent of tears.

"We'll just postpone it till the spring."

This only calms her down enough to sputter out, "If you don't marry me now, you never will."

"That's not true."

She recovers.

"I've got to get my head together," she says, pinching her eyes shut.

"We can get you into the best rehab on the planet, Lucille."

She wipes her eyes.

"I can't."

"The judge will like it. You know, show him you're serious about getting better."

"Not right now."

"Why not?"

She takes my hand and brings it to her breasts. She squeezes it as though words along cannot convey her depth of feeling and conviction, as though what she needs to communicate can only be transmitted by way of some synaptic pathway. "Day after tomorrow's my surgery," she whispers.

I look her in the eyes. "Postpone the surgery, Lucille."

"You can't postpone elective surgery. Not without paying for it—you know, it's like earnest money."

"You can postpone a marriage."

She pinches her eyes shut against the sound of my voice, as though this will cancel out all that has been said and done.

"I've worked so hard—all those double shifts…Let me do this one thing, then I'll do anything you ask. Anything."

The Other White Light

16

The decade of the seventies has been described by chroniclers of that time as an unlovely decade. Part of what made it so was the reemergence of cocaine, a drug that seems to breed garish self-love.

The cliches have survived: the narcissistic Peter Pan snorting a powder that inspires him to shake his booty through the night, the roller skating disco blockhead with the oversized pendant swinging from a gold necklace. Over the years cocaine came to be more broadly viewed as the drug of choice among the well-to-do, an emotional bulwark for the hollowed-out image of the decadent rich. It became fashionable, even among the sound-minded and less well-heeled. What isn't widely known is that the seventies and eighties was America's second cocaine epidemic.

Until 1858 cocaine could only be taken by chewing the leaves of cocoa bush, which produces an effect similar to that of drinking strong coffee. As a result there were few problems with addiction, as the method delivered the drug in tiny secretions through saliva. But in 1858 the German chemist Albert Niemann of the University of Gottingen isolated the active ingredient in the cocoa leaves and developed a method for extracting cocaine in an exceedingly pure form.

With no regulation and little understanding of the drug, cocaine quickly became popular in northern Europe and America. Indeed it was thought to be useful in a wide variety of medicinal capacities, while its downsides remained unknown. In the late nineteenth century doctors began prescribing it to patients as an anesthetic. According to biographer Peter Gay, Sigmund Freud, the founder of psychoanalysis, was not only a great proponent but a heavy user. He prescribed cocaine as a component of what he called the "talking cure," the very cornerstone of his breakthrough psychotherapy. By century's end, a full-blown cocaine epidemic was well underway in America, the drug everywhere. Until 1903 it was even in Coca Cola.

Over time, however, cocaine came to be seen as addictive and its users dangerous. What followed was the first-ever crackdown by the U.S. government on the drug trade, and an expressly effective one at that. By the time the Roaring Twenties came to its roaring conclusion, cocaine had effectively vanished from American society.

Signs of the second epidemic wouldn't reappear for another forty years—a long enough interval to erase the greater part of any memory of that ancient time when cocaine addicts broke into the local apothocary shop to get their fix. For most of the seventies cocaine was once again largely viewed as chic, fun, and harmless. It was also abundant.

Cocaine is made by harvesting cocoa leaves which are then crushed and mixed with a variety of petroleum-based chemicals, namely gasoline and kerosene. The process extracts the drug from the plant, leaving it in what is called a "freebase" form. Left like this, however, cocaine quickly loses its potency. To preserve it the paste is converted into a salt, which is the form doctors apply as a local anesthetic during minor surgeries, and recreational users snort and inject. To smoke cocaine it must first be converted back into the freebase form, which requires that it again be mixed with petroleum-based chemicals.

When cocaine came back into vogue in the seventies and eighties, it was used mainly in this salt form. That is, it was typically snorted, and occasionally injected by serious addicts. This salt-based mode of delivery became key to the popular fashion and the drug's greater allure, with people carrying vials of cocaine powder with them through their day. As with all illicit drugs, an esprit de corps developed among users, with vials, mirrors and gold-plated razor blades becoming part of the cocaine culture's patois.

This cocaine chic, vulgar as it was, would appear to have caught on in other drug circles, particularly among methamphetamine users. Suddenly, at the dawn of the eighties, in the midst of a great cocaine epidemic, the amphetamine pill all but evaporated. This old-fashioned drug that had been around all these years in tablet and bronchial inhaler form was broadly reinvented among those with lesser means as a powder drug to be chiseled against a mirror surface and snorted. Though hardly indistinguishable, the drugs are remarkably similar in appearance and stimulative effect. But the emulation wouldn't stop with the powder form of the drug.

In the 1960s the freebasing technique of cocaine began to surface among the most deeply addicted. The method wouldn't catch on for another decade, but once popular it immediately made national news when comedian Richard Pryor burned off the better part of his face while freebasing cocaine.

Methamphetamine users quickly took up smoking their drug of choice, creating a new and even more devastating mode of delivery than injection. The new form would have a seemingly benevolent or malevolent name depending upon how you looked at it. This smokeable methamphetamine would be called, simply, Ice.

17

Lucille emerges from the OR on a gurney, brain snowed with anesthesia, breasts neatly stitched in matching crescent moons about the nipples and wrapped in Ace bandages. Hours later, when she finally rouses herself, she begins to cry, softly and carefully so as not to draw too great a breath. I pet her head as she whimpers like wounded pup. Tears seep from the taut corners of her eyes.

Forty-eight hours later the bandages are removed so that she can view her new physique before a full-length mirror in our bedroom and inspect the trail of coarse black sutures. In her misery I witness a thrilling smile. She can't stop looking at herself, the feminine exaggeration of her outline. All she wants now as she draws the bandages back over herself is to be healed. But for now the pain is quite real.

In spite of all, I have come with my agenda. As she lay in bed I prepare to bring up the subject of rehab, a subject which has possessed me since the arrest. My line of reasoning is simple and practical. An incarcerated fiancée is not in the offing. Therefore she must do whatever is necessary to keep that from happening. Therefore she must get into a rehab program before she sets foot in a courtroom. Curry favor with the judge for all she is worth, demonstrate that she is well, at least well enough to understand she has a problem. She must keep her promise and do whatever I ask.

The unhandy timing of the proposition is gilded with a discovery, for I know of a less disruptive way of going about the whole process. In the newspaper I happened across an ad for an extended outpatient rehab program at a local hospital. I called for the brochure which sells the program as something like going to a job for eight hours a day, whereupon you return home in the evening. Lucille appears to consider this for a moment. Then she refuses, the grounds an unintelligible mutter. But it's the only strategy that might keep her out of the pokey and keep us together, and she knows it. I can see the wheels whirring in her head at impossible speeds before delivering her to the obvious conclusion.

The sessions begin a few days after she enrolls. There are a dozen other people from all walks of life in the class with some sort of drug dependency. In the beginning Lucille complains about the personal nature of the questions put to her by the therapist, someone she privately suspects of being a former addict, as he simply knows too much, and, in her opinion, knows it all too well. According to him the questions he poses are designed to open up those private compartments of memory that drugs and alcohol seal shut.

During the course of the sessions each "patient" is given a psychiatric evaluation, which, in Lucille's case, produces an unexpected result. One evening she comes home and says she has been diagnosed with a condition called borderline personality disorder, or BPD. I am concerned, but she is not. She doesn't know much about it and doesn't want to learn. Once I've asked too many questions, she merely hands me a pamphlet, which explains that seventy-five percent of the population with this disorder are women. They typically have trouble with personal relationships as they don't really see themselves as part of any community—be it family or a circle of friends. Nearly all have severe problems with drugs and alcohol. Most have a poor body image and are never satisfied with how they look. Reading on, it describes people with BPD as potential suicides, with a full ten percent succeeding in their attempt. An overwhelming majority of BPDs were sexually abused as children.

Lucille all over again. Looking over at her as she reads a paperback novel on the sofa, I'm suddenly taken by a sense of empathy and dread. When I ask Lucille about some of the unsettling statistics, she would seem to have no idea. No one has discussed the diagnoses with her at any length; she hasn't even read the pamphlet. With the mention of sexual abuse, she says she's going to turn in early.

Once she's gone, my mind is taken with mental portraits. Lucille the little girl. Lucille and the old men in her life. Lucille the adult in the act of perpetual escape.

The upshot in all of this is that the therapy would seem to be working. A new serenity descends upon daily life. Lucille comes home in the evening a little more buoyant than the day before. She's now collected, moving through her day with greater rudder. At first I suspect it might be a mere swelling of confidence, a sort of emotional counterpart to her surgery. But this seems to run deeper than that. She seems to have remembered who she once was. In the midst of this calm sea I call Dustin to tell him the news. His tone is subdued, gravely remorseful for having had even the most tangential role in Lucille's arrest. "The three of us go way back," he groans. "Remember that mansion I gave you guys the keys to all those years ago?"

"That's where the story began."

The conversation then strays for a while before inevitably returning to Lucille.

"She's in rehab eight hours a day, five days a week."

There's a pause.

"So it's outpatient rehab," he says.

"It's like going to a job every day."

After another curious pause I ask if anything's wrong.

"No, not really."

"What is it?"

He won't come out and say what's bothering him, but when I press him, he says in a muted tone, "Outpatient rehab has a mixed reputation."

"What's mixed about it?"

"It's thought to be for people who won't take the time to deal with their drug problem. They meet other serious drug addicts there, so it also turns out to be this place to network."

"I thought I was calling with good news."

"If you're serious about kicking a habit you don't enroll in outpatient rehab."

"I enrolled her," I say. "Sorry to report it's working."

"Sterling, nothing could make me happier than to see it work," he groans.

"Then you should be happy."

"That's great…it's just, I don't know…" Then, as though reciting a message baked in a fortune cookie, he says cryptically, "Beware of any new friends."

"Whose new friends?"

"Hers."

"I'm her only friend and she's sober as a nun."

"Well, that's the rap on outpatient rehab. Now I'll butt out."

I'm talking to a know-it-all. That, I want to say, is the rap on you, Dustin. A comfortable OBGYN flashing his street creds.

The conversation ends with an air of forced politeness, and in its calm wake I come to feel that I am the know-it-all. What I know is that I am good for Lucille.

The program quietly comes to a conclusion just as her court date arrives. Addressing the bar she looks like a million bucks, sharply dressed in a floral summer dress, big bosomed, confident, cheerful—a freshly tuned bride-to-be. Documents showing the voluntary nature of the enrollment and completion of an accredited drug rehab program are presented to the judge. He is visibly pleased, which he expresses in a motion to suspend the sentence of my fiancée's class four felony conviction.

A thousand maxims spring to mind. No risk, no reward. Never mind what people say. Trust your instincts. Don't let the bastards get you down. The one that rings truest of all is one of my own: Lucille needs me.

An Enduring Idea from the Haight

18

The world of drug laws is a world of unintended consequences. Nowhere has this been more apparent than in the government's attempts at getting a handle on the amphetamine and methamphetamine epidemics.

Government regulation of amphetamine put forth by the Kennedy administration hardly dented the supply of the drugs used for recreational purposes. The main culprits remained the pharmaceutical companies and physicians willing to produce and prescribe the drug, respectively, in vast quantities. As then-FDA Commissioner George Larrick testified to a House committee in 1965, "...our survey of production figures was incomplete because records kept by several basic manufactures were grossly inadequate, and also because two of the nation's largest pharmaceutical companies declined...to provide the information requested."

A few doctors in the San Francisco area were particularly complicit, as they began prescribing amphetamine injections for (incredibly) the treatment of heroin addiction. Restrictions for the pill form of amphetamine were not taken terribly seriously either for the balance of the decade. By then an especially unruly corner of the flourishing counterculture had developed a taste for the drug, producing a demand that could never be met by any company pretending to legitimacy. The injectable form became popular among serious users and a vacuum resulted—not from diminished supply but by soaring demand. The void would be filled in a most ominous manner, one that haunts the world today, one that has everything to do with the nature of methamphetamine, what sets it apart from every other family of drugs.

It's no secret that such phenomena are the products of market economies. Quite simply, where there is demand there will be a supplier to meet it. The principle that ruined Prohibition seemed to be lighting the kindling in the Haight-Ashbury District of San Francisco where there was an enormous population in a dangerously experimental mood.

During the mid—and late 1960s San Francisco's Haight-Ashbury district was transformed in the imaginations of millions of young people into a new kind of Promised Land, one that promoted the now-familiar stereotype of peace, free love, and an abundance of mind-altering drugs. A young physician by the name of Dr. David E. Smith practicing medicine there at the time characterizes the scene as the "the biggest drug taking culture in the history of human civilization." The drugs of choice were hallucinagenics, namely LSD and mescaline. But the source of the Haight's most serious problems lay with other compounds.

Just prior to what came to be known as "The Summer of Love," California fire departments began reporting something strange—a rash of explosions and fires in local residences tucked away in the hills of Northern California. Once extinguished, officials waded through the charred ruins of sophisticated labs containing the scorched remains of enormous triple-neck reaction vessels, Buchner funnels, separatory funnels, Bunsen burners, stashes of hydrochloric acid, sulfuric acid, acetone, benzyl chloride, methyl ethyl ketone, lead acetate, and a substance the name of which they could hardly pronounce. The latter-most was phenyl-2-propanone, also known as phenyacetone, or, as it would be widely called, P2P. P2P was not only legal but widely available as the active ingredient in a variety of cold medicines. Pharmaceutical companies had also been using it for years to make amphetamine and methamphetamine.

The portent for law enforcement lay in the reality that nothing in these burned out labs was a controlled substance. Indeed, none of it was really illegal until the process of cooking the methamphetamine was complete, which presented a legal challenge that did not apply to other drugs (you don't outlaw telephones because the Mafia uses them to conduct business, nor do you outlaw P2P because bad people might use it to make meth). Interdiction was also vastly complicated as the drugs were not being smuggled into the country, and the ingredients were not only here but here legally. In theory they could be legally put together so long as the chemist stopped one step shy of forming the first molecule of methamphetamine.

These clandestine labs were soon producing tremendous quantities of the liquid methamphetamine, the most dangerous and least available from pharmaceutical companies. In the main the labs were run by motorcycle gangs, namely the Hell's Angels. The meth hit the streets of Haight-Ashbury in substantial quantity at the middle of the decade, but its dramatic impact on the community wouldn't be fully felt for a few more years. To the mind of Dr. Smith its arrival meant the death of the idea of the sixties, the romantic image the decade aspired to be about.

Smith was perhaps the first to understand what everyone was seeing. Born in Bakersfield and educated at the University of California at Berkeley, he went on to medical school there where he specialized in pharmacology and toxicology. In 1965 he began research on amphetamine at the University of California at San Francisco General Hospital, working on a post-doctoral fellowship treating addiction. When he wasn't working, he went home to his Victorian home in the Haight. The distinction between work and home then began to blur.

One of his studies involved administering amphetamine to lab mice in escalating quantities until half of the mice died either by stroke or by cardiac arrest. The medical term for this dose is "medium dose lethal." The mice that survived were then placed in a cage with other mice that had also been given a medium dose lethal and survived, while a control group of mice were kept in a separate cage altogether. With this latter group all was perfectly serene. They ate their food, drank their water, and, significantly, groomed each other as good mice do. But Smith noticed something extraordinary occurring in the other cage. The amphetamine dosed mice there were attacking each other on a regular basis. Upon closer inspection, he noticed that the mice were interpreting normal grooming behavior as aggressive. In fact more mice were dying by attack rather than by seizure brought about by massive doses of the drug. The amount of amphetamine required to kill half of the mice in this manner is called the "aggregate amphetamine toxicity," and is a much smaller dose than the medium dose lethal. What the study indicated to Smith was that while all the variables were kept the same, the amount of drug required to kill by way of injury was substantially lower than what was required to kill by way of overdose. In time Dr. Smith could hardly fail to notice the unmistakable parallels between the mice in his lab and the people all around him on the streets of the Haight.

In 1967 most of the young people in the Haight-Ashbury District were still into LSD, mescaline and music. Indeed the psychedelic drugs seemed to be an intimate aspect of not only the music scene but the music itself. Experimental light shows that accompanied rock concerts by bands such as Jefferson Airplane, Janis Joplin, and the Grateful Dead sought to imitate an LSD trip. The concert gatherings, many of which were organized by Smith's friend, legendary promoter Bill Graham, were generally peaceful enough. During the latter half of the decade Smith began setting up free clinics in the Haight. These became the much-emulated Haight-Ashbury Free Clinics, which serve as primary care facilities for the uninsured, and deal to a large degree with the homeless and the addicted.

The clinics were born into a strange place and time, and saw more than their share of strange visitors. But one was particularly unforgettable. He had stringy black hair and a glowering stare, and was the leader of a motley group of hippies. Most striking, however, was the indelible swastika set into his forehead. His small group of followers, most of whom were women, were into LSD, and they had come, as so many other had, for the standing offer of free medical care. He called himself Charlie Manson.

Manson's arrival at the clinic could be interpreted as a portent of things to come. By the following summer, the summer of 1968, the Haight was beginning to change. This was the year that methamphetamine, arriving in massive quantities from the labs, made its impact felt. According to family member Susan Atkins, shortly after leaving San Francisco Manson and his family were said to have begun taking speed along with LSD. The combination would inflame the insanity that became the bloody madness of Helter Skelter.

The essence of the change in the decade's tone was somehow present in this bizarre carnage that captured world-wide attention. In Smith's words, "The dream of the sixties became a nightmare." Certainly there were manifold reasons for the developing madness, but the prevalence of methamphetmaine seems to have been widely overlooked.

Smith happened across another telling discovery. While working at the alcohol and drug screen unit at San Francisco General Hospital, he'd been conducting routine urine screens on patients in the psychiatric ward when it occurred to him that a full fifty percent of the patients diagnosed with paranoid schizophrenia tested positive for amphetamine use. Upon closer examination he concluded that these patients were not schizophrenic at all but suffering from amphetamine psychosis. That is, their auditory and visual hallucinations were not necessarily the product of the incurable mental illness but of heavy methamphetamine use. This was certainly good news, but still a serious problem, as these patients were receiving the wrong treatment and being given the wrong class of drugs. They didn't belong in the psyche ward but in a recovery program.

The discovery highlighted just how unprepared the medical community was for the amphetamine epidemic. So too was the rest of San Francisco society. "The kids who were into LSD and mescaline moved out, leaving the Haight to the speed freak," Smith says. Recalling a 1968 "60 Minutes" piece by correspondent Harry Reasoner, Smith says, "You could pick out the healthy kids in the footage shot on the street, and you could spot the speed freaks. Their behavior was that pronounced." This was the time of speed "shoot-ups" in Golden Gate Park, and the "Crystal Palace," a kind of needle-sharing ritual that involved young people shooting enormous quantities of liquid methamphetamine.

The following summer all of the elements made for another lethal mix at the Rolling Stones concert at Altmont Speedway in Livermore, California. On advice of the Grateful Dead, the decision was made to have security provided by the Hell's Angels. "It was supposed to be Woodstock West," Smith says. "But it was destroyed by speed."

While the Stones played "Under my Thumb," a Hell's Angel's biker knifed a young fan by the name of Meredith Hunter, killing him. Three other people also died at the concert from various causes.

The bizarre event was vaguely presented to the public as the bookend to an age of peace and love, evidence that the party of the sixties was over and that the hangover of the seventies underway. Rarely is methamphetamine's role ever mentioned.

19

Clyde sits on a metal folding chair in the ragged grass of his sideyard. He is surrounded by the dismantled ruins of four lawnmowers. At his side a cardboard box is piled with the machines' greasy viscera—a coiled starter cord, a throttle tab, lawnmower wheels, a blade, a fuel tank. Against it leans an engine block with a spark plug that has been beaten with a hammer, like a loose tooth impacted in a lower jaw. An array of dirty screwdrivers and a socket set are scattered before him. The tapered end of a chisel lies crosswise upon the handle of a ball-peen hammer. Clyde begins to tidy up his workspace as I approach, and then abruptly gives up. A weird frustration is revealed in a wide-eyed glare, a look of unfocused panic.

"What the hell are you doing, Clyde?" I say.

"Mower's on the fritz…f-f-ixing the fucking lawnmower."

"Didn't you once tell me you were a certified dozer mechanic?"

Deeply offended, he glowers at a pair of water-pump pliers.

"Making a mower that works out of four that don't takes something special, Mr. Braswell."

"You all right, Clyde?"

He cants his head and appears to give this question serious thought before answering. He then nods, stands, and quickly walks around the perimeter of his bizarre mess. "Whatcha come here for, Mr. Braswell?" he says as he studies his work, assesses his progress.

"The wedding's back on," I say.

"So I heard."

"I'm not going to be here to help with moving the cattle."

"Where's the wedding?"

"My parent's backyard."

"Where's the honeymoon?"

"Yucatan Peninsula."

Clyde nods.

"Colette and I are splitting up," he says, nearly stuttering the sentence. "She's g-getting the kids."

"Sorry to hear that," I mumble.

"Seventeen years and four kids later…" He drops an imaginary football, and then punts it. Looking down at his lawnmower carcasses, he shakes his head and adds, "What a cluster f-fuck."

◆   ◆   ◆

Greg and Earl stand before the bonfire, their faces aglow as I approach from the ranch house, a tray holding a bottle of Stoli, tonic water, cranberry juice, a carafe of chipped ice. It's July, too hot for a fire. The atmosphere is hushed, somehow a silent recognition that things aren't quite right, that some imprudent decisions have been made. Greg agrees that it's too hot for a fire. Earl would seem to concur.

"Think I'll be making a mistake tomorrow?" I toss the question out there if only to break up a cadence of awkward silences.

Greg clears his throat. "Why are you asking that question, Sterling? And why are you asking it now?"

I stare into the fire for a long while, hypnotized by the glowing coals.

"Just looking for some reassurance."

"She's been clean, hasn't she?" Earl says.

"Six months now."

"And you've known her for how long?"

"Twenty-some-odd years."

"Childhood sweethearts."

"She was great at last year's Fourth of July party," Greg says, laughing. "What with the hypodermic needles full of juice."

With that I feel myself getting drunk in a hurry. Then something strange happens. At some point deep in the night I find myself lying on the grass alongside the glowing coals, a trail of red ants traversing my ankle. Greg and Earl lie asleep on the lawn chairs, their legs akimbo at precisely the same angle.

I stagger to the house and collapse on the sofa. My mind hovers within that space between sleep and wakefulness until the sun has risen in the kitchen window. Then the phone rings. It's the florist with "a very important question for the groom." Seconds later it rings again and it's my mother. So the day instantly assumes a forward and unstoppable momentum of its own, as have the events that delivered me to this peculiar point in time.

The morning of August 21, 1999 breaks hot and humid. Time becomes elastic with the injection of vodka, allowing Greg, Earl and myself to arrive at my parents' home an hour late with a luminous sense of sangfroid. The guests are seated, the quartet's bows drawn. Lucille is said to be in my parents' bedroom announcing to all who enter that she's *"living the highlife now!"* I am warned away in the interest of fortune and tradition. In the kitchen I overhear Lucille's mother's latest husband whispering between themselves "…she looks fine…"

"Do you think it will last?"

The answer is so hushed as to be inaudible.

I turn on my heel and head outside where a pair of teal-colored dragonflies are buzzing up and down the aisle. Everyone is hot, drunk and fairly miserable. The dragonflies eventually light on my seven-year-old niece's naked shoulder, sending her screaming into the neighbor's arboretum. A moment later I am directed down the aisle. From the dais I see Lucille for the first time in three days. When she finally stands before me and the veil lifted, I am overwhelmed by a sense of relief that she is present, fully living in the hear-and-now. As if I should have expected anything else, as if anxious behavior were not normal on a bride's wedding day.

A scalding sun and a steady trickle of alcohol through the reception are replaced that evening by a jet ride and then a cool breeze coming off the Mexican Caribbean. We sit in chaise lounges as the final rays of sunlight illuminate the brain-shaped cumulus clouds in panels of pink and violet. Lucille lies at my side, eyes wide open as though scanning the skies for UFOs. She swears she feels fine, but "something's a little freaky."

"What do you mean by 'something's a little freaky'?"

She looks me dead in the eyes, and says cryptically, "Baby, you don't know what's going on in your own backyard, do you?"

I shake my head and lie back down. Soon we're off to the hut, lying beneath the ceiling fan, listening to the sea moving against the endless expanse of coral sand. Lucille reaches over and takes me in her hand, a quiet moment that is followed by a session of absolutely furious sex. In the sweaty aftermath we both lie awake, not talking much. A faint pall of foreboding fills my head. I ponder what Lucille meant by her curious statements, but I'm afraid to ask, cautious of any scenes on our wedding night. In time my mind strays. Finally I dream.

The days are spent within the refuge of the beach umbrella and fueled by a steady stream of daiquiris from the thatched-roof wet bar a hundred yards off. Days and nights dovetail seamlessly until the morning Lucille announces that she's making a taxi run into town for some contact lens solution. While she's gone I head back to our cabin and happen to notice a notepad jutting out of her suitcase. Ah, the relentless companion, the prescription pad.

I retreat to the shade of the beach, the breeze, the daiquiris. A couple hours later Lucille appears above me wearing a pink string bikini. Looking up at her she suddenly appears grotesquely skinny, her tendons and bones unwholesomely prominent. Not everyone is of the same opinion. A German tourist in a Speedo gawks lewdly at Lucille as his wife swats a mosquito against the tremendous corpulence of her thigh.

"You brought a prescription pad," I say.

"And it's a good thing because I have a bladder infection."

"Thought you were just getting saline solution."

"Got that too."

"Anything else?"

Lucille grimaces.

"You know, they don't check tourists coming into Mexico," I add. "But they check everyone one on the way back."

"Why are you telling me this?"

"Just reciting useful facts."

Lucille turns her gaze to the sea.

"You drink like a porpoise."

"So?"

"Just reciting a useful fact."

The following Sunday we're on our way to the airport. As we approach the ticket counter, Lucille stops, closes her eyes, and then abruptly darts off to the ladies room, trailing her wheeled suitcase. A moment later she reappears. We then board a planeload of sunburned and hungover Texans, and soar over the Gulf for Houston.

Upon deplaning we are escorted as a group to the baggage carousel. Just as our luggage tumbles down, Customs officials being led by two Labrador retrievers approach. They seem preternaturally drawn to Lucille, the dogs' noses zigzagging through the crowd, eventually coming right up to her ankles. Lucille stands rigid, arms at her side, forehead and shoulders glistening with perspiration. A dog's shiny black snout comes around her heel, up her shin, then shoots off for her suitcase. It then moves the entire length of the zipper, pauses, then comes all the way around Lucille. I gaze at her brittle posture, and she at me. She mouths, "Take me with you," and, just as before, all her weaknesses fall away, all her strange misdemeanors and sins forgiven. Lucille needs me. Nonetheless, the dog has clearly detected something—and yet I can't imagine she has anything on her. If she was holding, she isn't now. The official allows the retriever to linger, to do her job carefully. Lucille's eyes well up, and just as she's about to break down, the Lab turns her nose to another bag, another person.

So we have our luggage and Lucille her freedom.

"What was the dog was picking up?" I ask as we walk for the terminal.

Lucille shrugs.

"Traces of something. You were scared, Lucille."

She will neither confirm nor deny. She takes my hand and says, her voice atremble, "Just get me out of here."

Looking at her profile as we walk, I see the corner of her eye seeping a long tear.

Proliferation and Mutation

20

By the dawn of the new decade there were two distinct varieties of amphetamine addicts—one old, one new, and neither having much in common with the other.

What's important is the central idea that, in general, the older set did not see *themselves* as part of the drug culture. Indeed they were, as a group, innately averse to it. Although defined as being otherwise law abiding, these old-fashioned amphetamine addicts had their dark actors.

The darkest of them arrived in the San Francisco Bay area in 1965. His name was Jim Jones, and he was said to be the head of a small, controversial congregation from Indiana. He had brought 140 of his followers here because he was certain that a nuclear holocaust was imminent, and he'd read that the town of Ukiah in Mendicino County, California, would be safe when the inevitable happened. Unfortunately for Jones, a man distinctly prone to bouts of paranoia, his new home happened to be awash in a drug that would not serve his nature and particular state of mind very well.

His church, which he called "The People's Temple," grew quickly over the next few years, and consisted largely of blacks and the poor. His doctrine was a mixture of Christianity and socialism, with a strong dose of anti-establishment sentiment. As the church grew, Jones became a familiar figure in mainstream San Francisco politics, Left-leaning as they were. United States Congressmen Phillip and John Burton, Assemblyman Willie Brown, and Mayor George Moscone all sought assistance from Jones who gladly delivered votes and thousands of volunteers to help campaign on a moment's notice. In retrospect it seems incredible, but in October of 1976 Mayor Moscone actually named Jim Jones to a seat on the San Francisco Housing Authority Commission.

Jones's behavior was oftentimes bizarre, and didn't entirely escape scrutiny from the local and regional press. During church services Jones reportedly performed miracle "cancer healings" which were obviously faked, and it was learned through defectors of the church that many of his followers had suffered beatings at the hands of Jones and those in his inner-circle. Jones's paranoia and burgeoning megalomania became more pronounced as his daily intake of Quaaludes and amphetamines increased through the years. Whenever he appeared in public he was surrounded by bodyguards, and then came talk of building a People's Tem-

83

ple "commune" in the jungles of Guyana, a small South American country. Here his followers would be promised a new life, one free of the persecution inflicted upon them in America.

In spite of negative publicity, Jones's church continued to grow. By 1973 the People's Temple opened the doors of a sister church in Los Angeles, and the following years Jones was granted permission by the government of Guyana to begin construction of the commune on a remote 300-acre parcel of land near the Venezuelan border. In August of 1977 he and his followers moved to their jungle outpost, which came to known as "Jonestown." During the course of the next year the population would come to exceed 1,000 people.

According to a federal report on Jones and his People's Temple, Jones had a physician who would prescribe to him amphetamine on demand. The doctor also saw that shipments of barbiturates were sent down to Jonestown on a regular basis. The amphetamines were for Jones, the barbiturates for his followers. The amphetamines fueled endless sermons broadcast over a loudspeaker system; all the while, the drinking water was being laced with the barbiturates, which Jones believed would make his followers more compliant. In spite of the barbiturates, however, complaints emerged from the jungle and made their way back to the United States.

In June of 1978 a Jonestown defector by the name of Deborah Layton was interviewed by the San Francisco *Chronicle*. Layton described the jungle outpost as a place of public beatings and mass suicide drills. In response to concerns from relatives of Jonestown residents, U.S. Representative Leo Ryan of San Mateo announced plans to visit Jonestown to investigate. While there in November of 1978 some of the residents secretly passed notes to Ryan expressing their wish to leave with him. When Ryan finally did leave, he and his party were mowed down by automatic rifle fire before their plane as it idled on the tarmac. But this was only the beginning of the madness.

Simultaneous to the shooting, Jones announced over the loud speaker system that the American government was coming to destroy him and anyone involved with the People's Temple. He then instructed his followers to drink a cyanide-laced concoction. At 5:00 p.m. on November 18, 1978 the mass suicide commenced, with nearly everyone complying. Early the next morning Guyanese rescue forces arrived at Jonestown where they discovered 914 dead. Among them was the body of Jim Jones. Upon closer examination it became clear that small children were given injections of cyanide, and those who refused were simply shot and killed.

The role of amphetamine in the Jonestown tragedy should perhaps be viewed in the same light as Hitler's use of the drug. That is, amphetamine only influenced two minds prone to paranoia and delusion, in both cases magnifying personal tendencies of aggression and self destruction.

First and foremost, it should be noted that amphetamine itself killed no one in the Jonestown tragedy; cyanide did, and no one blames that drug for the hundreds of deaths. And yet it is difficult to fathom this outcome without amphetamine coursing through the veins of the architect of this uniquely twentieth century nightmare. Indeed, the drug's fingerprints are everywhere—from Jones's paranoid, delusional thinking to the megalomania to the mass murder that seems so strangely inevitable in retrospect.

From this point of view, the parallels to Hitler's amphetamine use, the Holocaust, and his eventual suicide would seem legitimate, for it appears plausible that in both cases amphetamine enhanced each man's weakness for epic violence and escape by way of apocalypse. Homicidal dimensions are magnified by this strange crystalline powder. In such bloody aftermath, suicide appears an acceptable, if not the only way out for its charismatic host.

◆   ◆   ◆

By the end of the sixties nearly everyone in the Bay area was, in Dr. Smith's words, "taking something." Few gave much thought to the consequences. For young people in other corners of the country, and indeed around the world, San Francisco was their cultural Mecca, as much a state of mind as a place. And thus a pandemic like no other was well underway, with tens of millions of people in their formative years experimenting with every kind of mind-altering compound.

The phenomenon, however, wouldn't go entirely unchecked. A consensus gradually developed on Capital Hill that something had to be done at the federal level about illicit drug use, something on the same grand scale as the epidemic. And so it was with landmark legislation rendered in the form of the Controlled Substance Act of 1970. The CSA, as it would come to be known, was the legal foundation of the federal government's mandate to stem what appeared to be an unstoppable tide.

Amphetamine in its various forms were officially placed on what was called "Schedule II" of the CSA. Of the five schedules of controlled substances, the second merely indicates that the drug has a high potential for abuse, but also legitimate medical uses. Abuse of a schedule II drug may lead to severe psychological or physical dependence. Other schedule II drugs such as cocaine and codeine, for example, are used in various medications to control pain. Of course amphetamine has legitimate medical uses such as for weight control and attention deficit disorder, hence its placement. According to the CSA, Schedule I drugs have a high potential for abuse but no accepted medical use—drugs such as heroin and mescaline. The scheduling of substances, however, would prove eternally controversial with drugs like marijuana being relegated to Schedule I for its actual or perceived lack of medical usefulness to the mind of the American medical establishment. But as Dr. Smith points out, "there's nothing inherently evil about a molecule."

Amphetamine's placement on Schedule II had a profound effect on how it would be come by in the future. First and foremost, it severely curtailed federally approved production quotas of amphetamine and methamphetamine by drug companies, and forced them to pull injectable liquid products from the shelf altogether. Mainstream America could still get amphetamines in pill form from their doctors, but only in very limited quantities. Mexico would help fill the vacuum among the most ardent fans of pep pills, which gained infamy on the street as "Cartwheels" or "White Crosses." They were still cheap, though not as ridiculously so as they were in the early sixties. A decade later one could still come by a hundred tablets for five or ten dollars, while today a single tablet costs one to five dollars.

The habits of the younger archetype of the amphetamine user was left largely untouched by the CSA. Speed labs need only raw materials, all of which could be bought legally from wholesalers and local retail stores.

By the time the CSA came into effect, the bristling mood of the Haight-Ashbury District had swept up and down the West Coast like waves of bad weather. The mood was preceded by the subtle installation of a speed lab. In the national media, the problem was characterized as being a problem unique to "Coastal California," a phenomenon limited to the absurd street theatre of that famously eccentric state.

For the chemist of the clandestine lab legal obstacles remained remarkably few for a remarkably long period of time. For decades the principle problem would merely be a matter of knowing where to come by the ingredients. According to Will Glaspy, a former DEA agent who worked meth cases in Southern California, "You could literally walk into a chemical supply company with a recipe for methamphetamine, hand them the recipe, and tell them: 'Give me everything on that list so that I can manufacture methamphetamine.'" Though not exactly *legal* to do this, Galspy says, neither were the laws developed enough at the time to make it decidedly *illegal.* Such legislation wouldn't come onto the books until late the following decade.

Until then law enforcement had to resign itself to working within the existing, albeit inadequate, legal framework. But there were tactics that could be adopted; all that was required was an understanding of the phenomenon, how this methamphetamine actually came into being. In numerous cases, according to Glaspy, DEA agents would set up surveillance at a chemical supply companies and wait for a methamphetamine chemist to come in and "fill up his El Rancho with all the glassware and chemicals that he needed, and then follow him back to his home. Three days later he'd have methamphetamine." If the arrest was made too early or late, all was for naught. Although such tactics bred some success, the whole charade highlighted the unique and perhaps insurmountable obstacles in controlling the drug in the years to come.

It wasn't until 1980 that P2P itself was placed in Schedule II of the Controlled Substance Act. The result was a decline in lab seizures, but the decline was brief. Its brevity was the result of the street chemists' innovations. In the wake of the scheduling came the decade of the eighties, the decade thought to be the sire of the modern meth epidemic, the one we recognize today. According to the DEA more than 400 labs were seized in 1987. But one was different from all the rest. Upon close inspection agents saw that this lab was the first of its kind to use a new precursor chemical, a substitute for P2P. This new lab employed what was known as the hydriodic acid/ephedrine reduction method, which is considerably simpler than any that came before. Just as P2P had been a decade earlier, ephedrine was still unregulated.

The drug has been around for millennia. More than five thousand years ago the Chinese revealed the stimulant properties of the mahuang plant, known in the West as the ephedra plant from which ephedrine is derived. Ephedra's recent history is more controversial, as it has been the active ingredient in various "food supplements" marketed to athletes and people who just want to lose weight. But ephedrine has a long medical history here in the United States as well. For decades ephedrine had been used by pharmaceutical companies as the active ingredient in bronchial dilators to treat asthma. Since ephedrine is not produced in the United States, it had to be imported—and in tremendous quantities—from abroad by operators of clandestine labs. For years the importation was entirely legal.

An omen could be read in the tea leaves. Purity of the drug was on the rise as meth cooks refined their skills: in the early seventies the purity of seized methamphetamine averaged thirty percent; by 1983 average purity had reach sixty percent. Perhaps it seemed innocuous at the time, but to Glaspey's mind, the ethereal ingredient of knowledge was the true menace of the methamphetamine epidemic. And it had a lower common denominator than anyone thought possible. Chemistry would prove to be an imminently creative science, capable of being dumbed-down to a level understood by fry-cooks. What if some inspired Doctor Morell developed a recipe for making meth from a beaker of sand and water? And what if he could teach any but the most simple-minded to make it?

According to Glaspey, this was precisely the direction things seemed to be proceeding by the late 1980s. But problems for law enforcement were now compounded by underground research and development of entirely new drugs. Someone somewhere (some say China, others Korea) came up with a smokeable form of methamphetamine, the dextro isomer methamphetamine, which proved to be extremely potent and wildly popular in Hawaii and on the West Coast. For a while it seemed little more than a fad that went by various names such as "glass," "batu," and "shabu." As a result of this spike in popularity it cost more, although the process for making Ice is a relatively straightforward process of converting methamphetamine into a crystal. Profits exploded as addiction proliferated beyond anyone's worst dream. When Ice is smoked it almost instantly enters the bloodstream and finds its way to the brain. It's similar in effect to injecting meth, and far more potent than any oral dose. Its power lay in the "d." The manufacturing process produces the stereochemically pure d-isomer, the most active form of methamphetamine.

The effects of the drug are much like those experienced by smokers of crack cocaine. The high from Ice, however, lasts anywhere from eight to twenty-four hours, whereas a typical crack high lasts twenty minutes. The crime Ice inspires is phenomenally violent, as the user typically becomes paranoid, suffering from both auditory and visual hallucinations.

The manifestation of Ice completed methamphetamine's parallel with cocaine, as it had been typically snorted and injected. Now it could be smoked, just like crack. Clearly a great many methamphetamine users were engaged in the sincerest form of flattery.

21

The first trading days of the new millennium bring new highs for company stock listed on the New York Stock Exchange and NASDAQ in spite of a landmark antitrust suit brought by the U.S. Department of Justice. Seven days later our stock price begins to slip a few points. Court rulings are handed down against the company, and the stock price continues to slide a little further. What only a few have predicted is that it won't stop sliding for twelve months, and when it finally does stop it will be worth but a third of its prior value. This means that I too will be worth but a third of what I was a year ago. Thank you, Madame General. Thank you, Judge Jackson.

The atmosphere at work slowly morphs from typical merry optimism to gloom, a mood that seems to follows me from work to home. Lucille quits her job at the height of the market, and marvels at my anxiety over the dismal course of the year. When she asks why I'm suddenly watching our expenses, I merely gesture at the red stock ticker zipping along at the base of the screen on CNBC, the grainy image of my boss being deposed on videotape.

I now work all the time, as new market conditions require the company to do more with less. Lucille occupies herself with the ranch, while her ties to the city life she once relished diminish. In retrospect the motives behind the change are plainly clear. She seems to be always awake, making a run to Seven/Eleven for a Slurpy at three in the morning, and when I see her on the weekends, her patience is on the wane. She has a new life of constant leisure and play and cannot summon much in the way of good cheer. The grating new attitude is, to my naïve mind, inexplicable. She no longer has access to pharmaceuticals; her name written in the pharmaceutical world's computer network, chiseled in binary stone. When I happen across her prescription pad, I see that she's now using it as a shopping list, its ordained use abandoned. She doesn't appear at all high—that is, she doesn't slur her words, her thinking is reasonably cogent. It's the kind of mystery that preoccupies the mind, never let's me completely relax, makes me think I'm missing something important here—perhaps love's hot fire has cooled in her heart. And yet to inquire is to court Armageddon.

In March of 2000 I take the weekend off from work and head up to the ranch. Lucille and Emily have been there for two weeks now, but when I arrive that Friday evening the door is unlocked, lights on, the house empty. On the countertop is a hastily scrawled sticky note from Lucille saying Emily has a slight fever, that she has taken her to the pediatrician in Houston. I look around the living room, out the windows at the rainy darkness. So I'll be spending the weekend alone.

The early afternoon is spent clearing brush, and later mending fence along the road to the ranch. In the midst of stretching a line of broken wire a Honda Accord that has been beaten to hell suddenly slows as it passes, as though the driver recognizes me. Then it races off.

That evening I fix a drink, put on some dour R&B, and take a seat in a lawn chair to watch the sun set. Just as it drifts into the trees I hear a car pulling onto the wash-gravel drive. A car door opens and slams shut, the gate squeals open. When I come around to the front of the house I see the Honda that drove by so slowly a few hours earlier. A woman approaches in the half-light, and says, "Are you Sterling Braswell?"

"I am. Who are you?"

"Colette Pierson," she says. "Clyde's wife. You have a minute?"

"All the time in the world."

We head inside to the kitchen where I fix Colette a vodka and tonic and express my condolences on their imminent divorce.

She doesn't possess, it would seem, the typical hallmarks of the church-going wife and mom. She chugs her drink like it was lemonade, every now and then releasing an expletive in regard to her soon-to-be ex-husband, that "piece of shit," that "toothless fucking hillbilly." Nor does she look like a woman I would figure for Clyde Pierson's wife of seventeen years. The contradictions begin with her looks. She's pretty. Wrangler boot-cut jeans, lace-up cowboy boots, a t-shirt that's modest but just clingy enough to hint at a lovely shape. She also comes off with an air of wryness, which suggests that she's smart in a way that extends well beyond mere common sense. She cannot be, I tell myself, married to Clyde.

I offer her a seat at one end of the sofa, and I take a seat at the other. She then draws a deep breath and begins to say what she "came here to say." I am all ears, I remark.

"You and I have two people in common," she begins.

"Who's that?"

"Clyde and Lucille."

"I didn't know you two were acquainted."

"I know everyone Clyde's slept with."

She watches my mouth slowly arc into a grin.

"And that's just the beginning," she adds after allowing for a long silent moment. "You're in for a show-stopper, Sterling."

"Your former husband calls me 'Mr. Braswell.'"

"And he's been carrying on with your wife," she says evenly.

"So what else did you come here to say?"

"Lucille was like a doctor, wasn't she?"

"What does this have to do with anything?"

"She could write her own prescriptions, right?"

"Get to your point, Colette."

"Then she got caught at the Kroger."

I give nothing away, but merely reflect her strangely ironic gaze.

"She was caught," she continues quite slowly, like a student reciting a list of facts committed to memory, "and now she can't buy *toothpaste* from a pharmacy."

"How do you know any of this?"

"So she like had to come up with her own pharmacy…or someone or something who could do what that scribbled little note used to do." Colette's brown weathered fingers dance about either side of her long tendrils. "Somebody like Clyde and his magic chemistry set."

"And where is this magic chemistry set of his?"

"Oh, maybe on a great big ranch where the owner's hardly ever around and the clueless neighbors won't pick up a nasty stench."

"And what does Clyde's chemistry set make?"

She smiles, parts her hands, and says, "Good ol' fashioned methamphetamine!"

In spite of Colette's intelligence, something about her worldly-wise demeanor compels one to disbelieve her. About her is an air of the small town conspiracy theorist, the meddling neighbor who has the low-down on the gypsy family down the street. Her thin lips smile as she implies that my wife has been unfaithful, that she is involved in a scheme in which Lucille exchanges sex for drugs with a man who looks like a hyena. For some reason she thinks it best to tell me this with so much certainty and lightness, as though she were confiding in me at a kitchen table over a hand of old maid cards. She doesn't see the tremendous gravity of her accusations, which, I remind myself, should only undermine the veracity of the accusations themselves. Of course their fantastic nature affirm in my mind the depths of Colette's deluded state.

"You look like someone who doesn't believe any news but good news," she says.

"I have a weakness for plausibility, Colette."

Her eyes swing pendulously from left to right, right to left in mock contemplation. Then she snickers, "So you're saying you don't believe me? Or you do..."

I come to my feet and part my hands in an expansive gesture of frankness. "Colette, my wife has her share of problems, but they aren't necessarily mixed up in *your* problems. Now if you wouldn't mind getting the hell out of here."

The insolent smile is still there, the rocking eyes following the interior carom of menacing thoughts.

"Think how surprised you'd be if everything I said was true," she says.

"No need to dump your domestic trash in my living room, Colette. I understand. You are getting divorced. You're bitter."

"But you see, it's all one big trash pile."

"Leave now."

She drains her glass as she comes to her feet. She then stands and wags her hips as she heads out the door and into the night. Her car starts in the darkness, and is gone.

That night I go to bed with drunk, uneasy thoughts. Deep in the morning the phone rings. "Is Lucille there?" a husky woman's voice asks.

"No she's not," I grunt, "and it's four in the morning."

"Tell her Tanya called when she gets back," and the phone goes dead.

I stare through the darkness at the glowing receiver in my hand. Who the hell is Tanya?

In the morning the uneasy thoughts linger, nagging the ancient, ever-vigilant part of the brain that silently insists all is not well. Sitting at the breakfast table before an overcooked Denver omelet I decide that what's needed is company. The weight of cabin fever must be offset. A party is in order. I punch out the numbers to home in Houston and get Lucille on the line. She's all for a party. Emily isn't so sick after all; she'll park her with her grandparents for a few days and drive on up. Then I mention my conversation with Colette.

"Colette who?" she says.

"Clyde's wife,"

"Clyde who?"

"Nevermind. A woman by the name of Tanya called at four in the morning."

"Thanks."

"Who's Tanya?"

"Somebody I met in rehab who's *always* needing moral support."

The conversation ends on that note. I remind myself that I am in search of company, and within a half-hour I've made a dozen phone calls with commitments from a dozen coworkers to make the drive up or down or over from Houston, Dallas and Austin. Within a few hours slightly dated sports cars begin a steady promenade through the gate to the ranch. The degree of willingness of everyone to scratch work plans on such short notice speaks to the overwhelming desire of all to blow off steam. The ranch, they know, is the place, for a bawdy reputation precedes it.

Lucille arrives at dusk in an uneven mood. She steps from the car yammering incessantly about dual-lane traffic, croupy children, uncooperative grandparents. When she finally pauses to breathe, she says, "Looking forward to some fun."

I throw up my hands in a gesture of surrender. "That's what we're all here for."

I am rewarded with a peck on the cheek. She then swings her small sporty dufflebag about her shoulder and trots off for the noisy crowd gathered in the kitchen.

The night is a series of bitter conversations about declining stock prices, impending layoffs, devastated 401k portfolios. Lucille watches on as these people she once knew as high-tech kingpins drown their sorrows in bourbon and vodka. Swaggering confidence has given way to diffidence and brooding over what might have been, over the Department of Justice, a spinster from the Sunshine State, a judge who has yet to send his first email, a nineteenth century idea called antitrust that has pauperized the lot of us. I quietly watch Lucille as she listens in on a conversation between two former millionaires. Looking at her anonymously in profile she appears disgusted, impatient with the circumstances of my coworkers. She listens but says nothing. I recognize the curl of her upper lip, the drawn eyes. Pure contempt.

As I'm watching her I feel a sharp tap on my shoulder. I turn about to see Clyde grinning at me. His clothes are clean, his jeans new, hair shiny with pomade. I'm thinking, This is the first time I've seen you in a shirt with a collar.

"Saw you were having a party and wondered why I wasn't invited," he hollers over the booming music.

"It was all spur-of-the-moment," I shout. "Say, your wife paid me a visit last night."

"She's nuts."

"She is."

"Where can I find myself a drink around here?"

I point to the kitchen counter where a rampart of liquor bottles stands. At that point we part ways, and I end up launching the remains of the fireworks leftover from that memorable Fourth of July. Lucille and her hypodermic needles, her cache of medicines, the world of safe and legal. The fireworks bloom overhead in globes of colored light as my mind momentarily trips backward.

Later in the night I wander back to the house to refill my drink, my back getting slapped everywhere I go. Computer geeks like it out here. Lots of booze and no technology. As I walk my bladder alarm sounds, and I head to the bathroom off the master bedroom. A seam of light and a groan indicate it's in use, so I just stand and wait in the darkness. Then comes another groan, this time from a woman, and I'm thinking it's being used well.

An awareness dawns as disparate suspicions coalesce in the moment...*you don't know what's going on in your own backyard...the man with the magic chemistry set...an unannounced presence...the abandoned prescription pad...a mental picture of my emaciated wife*...I approach the door, my mind churning in a wave of sickening panic. The doorknob turns freely in my grip, the door swings open. The vanity light bears down on Lucille's black hair as it pours over her head, shrouding her face. Clyde's eyes momentarily go wide as he thrusts himself away from the small of Lucille's arched back. His pecker gleams in the harsh light as he struggles to yank up his starchy new jeans. Lucille turns to me and shouts, *"It's not what you think, baby!"*

I look down at the vanity counter and see a pile of yellow-white powder on a picture of Lucille and me on the beach during our honeymoon. Pink clouds, turquoise sea. Upon my face a razor blade stands lodged in a solid chunk of crystal. Then comes the other staggering sight.

Turning to Clyde, I see that he's waving a pistol like he's playing a part in a bad western.

"Guess we'll be going now, Mr. Braswell," he says as he blindly reaches for Lucille's wrist. Incredibly, she lets him take it. He then leads her out of bathroom like she is a little girl and he her daddy, a reincarnated stepfather.

"Just let go of her, Clyde," I say calmly.

"It's not what you think," Lucille says, the words trailing over her shoulder again and again as she's pulled along. They move through the kitchen and living room where my drunken friends drink and smoke, oblivious of what's going on. My eyes meet Lucille's for the briefest moment.

"What the hell are you doing?" I shout over the noise. *"Where are you going?"*

She shakes her head as though confused. The music is so loud and here she is being led away by my employee who has a gun. Her expression is one of reluctant compliance, a damsel in mock distress. Looking back at me, she knows (just *knows!*) I have misinterpreted what I have seen tonight. She loves me *so much* (do I even understand how much she loves me?), but she's helpless...

"This is insane, Lucille!" I yell.

When they reach the front door Clyde hurls it open, and the two dash away. Clyde's truck turns over, and then spins furiously through the wash gravel for the road. I stand in the darkness, staring at the ruby glow in the trail of dust, suddenly taken by an eerie calm. Everything feels so real, so lifelike; but surely this is a dream...

My project coordinator approaches me where I stand in the front yard. Apparently he's the only one to have noticed that Clyde had a gun and that he left with my wife.

"What the hell just happened?" he says, utterly blown away.

"Lucille's having problems," is all I say. This is a side of my life that I wasn't aware of sixty seconds ago; now that I am aware, I wish only that it remain private. Turning to face him, however, I see that this bizarre event has had a transcendent effect. Suddenly I am a mild-mannered techie living The Wild Life. Booze, guns, women, computers—all of the elements in life that he covets.

"Wow," he says rather drunkenly. "Crazy man with a firearm. Takes off with your woman."

"That's about it, John."

"Is Lucille also a crazy person?" he says, careful so as not to sound flippant.

"I'm afraid so."

"Should we call the police?"

I consider this for a moment, then imagine Lucille being pulled over with a pound of meth in her purse. And who knows what Clyde would be capable of were he faced with the prospect of imminent arrest.

"Don't call the police," I say

In as sober a voice as he can muster, John asks, "So what does the situation call for?"

It calls for everyone to go home. That's what I want to say. But it's late and everyone is drunk and miles from their beds. So I say what he wants to hear.

"The situation, John, calls for a drink."

My back is then slapped with manly enthusiasm.

"It ain't a party till somebody shows up with a gun!" he shouts as though her were a cowboy and not a project coordinator for a colossal software company.

In time a drink is presented, and the music turned way, way up. At that point I slip outside and sit within the shadow of a remote locust tree, shivering with what I can only describe as an electric panic.

My girl is gone. My god, she is gone.

Two friends from the networking division stagger by, ice cubes jingling against their glasses.

"That you, Sterling?" one of them asks.

"Sterling?" says the other.

A whispered exchange, and they walk off. Then in the distance, their voices magically mingle with the pop and crackle of the bonfire: "...just a total breakdown...fucking *scary*..."

Research and Development

22

The early incarnations of the methamphetamine street chemists were a far cry from the meth cooks of today. The former were not only smart but arguably brilliant. Surely some must have learned their craft in the world of legitimate chemistry and pharmacology, only to lose their way experimenting with means and methods of brewing a wide variety of methamphetamines and what would come to be known by their eerily modern rubrics of "analogue," or "designer" drugs, such as MDE, MDA, MDMA, MDME. What they accomplished by sheer dint of nefarious wit, scientific ingenuity and marketing savvy is nothing short of astonishing. Indeed, their achievements were as unprecedented as they were devastating.

Their work had to take into account not only chemistry, but *brain* chemistry—scientific considerations which had to come in line with legal and marketplace realities. To become a true phenomenon a process had to be developed that produced the drug in quantity with relative ease, and it had to be so good that those who took it up would never want to quit. And that's exactly what they accomplished. Their entrepreneurial spirit even took it a step or two further, attracting a far larger customer base with a variety of products.

Methamphetamine works at the most basic level of pleasure by increasing the levels of dopamine in the brain. Dopamine is a neurotransmitter that acts as the currency of the brain's own reward system. Whenever we work hard and achieve a goal, the brain releases dopamine, and we experience a high, natural satisfaction. After a relatively brief period of time the high naturally and gradually dissipates, returning us to the realm of everyday life. Methamphetamine tampers with this most basic mechanism, essentially spiking the system with dopamine without any hard work, artificially creating intense feelings of euphoria and general well-being. For good measure, it then blocks the "re-uptake" of dopamine in the cerebral cortex and limbic areas of the brain. In effect, dopamine is secreted into the system and is then made to stay there.

Unlike other stimulants, methamphetamine also blocks the metabolism of these neurotransmitters by the body. According to researchers at the National Institute on Drug Abuse (NIDA), this is why the effects of the drug last so much longer than, say, cocaine. It remains in the blood stream virtually unchanged for an enormous stretch of time, giving it a half-life of ten to twenty hours instead of perhaps an hour or two.

Nevertheless all highs are ephemeral, even an amphetamine high, and the drug is inevitably purged from the body. But the brain is a stern governor. Over the course of months and years the heavy user's brain begins to produce less and less dopamine, as it wearies of the hyper-stimulation. According to drug rehabilitation specialists, this is why the methamphetamine addict feels the tremendous depression for many months after he stops using—hence the tremendously high rate of relapse among those trying to quit. When he can no longer stand the deprivation, the world becomes a sleepless place of incessant anxiety, paranoia and violence. And there seems to be no way out of the nightmare. In these haunted realms it is unfathomable that this amphetamine dreamworld is apocryphal, a tempest of mere molecules coursing through a stormy vault of consciousness.

Incredibly, the dream itself can be chemically altered. One of the most striking features of amphetamine is the ability of its molecular structure to be tailored, producing a wide variety of effects. Some are more hallucinogenic, others more stimulative, some merely producing a sense of heightened empathy, while others are a blending of all these effects. One of the reasons for this capacity is, in part, the ability of Mother Nature to produce right-and left-handed molecules, or molecules that are mirror images of themselves (bear in mind that these are not identical molecules, and indeed they have dramatically different psychoactive properties). "Ice," or dextro isomer methamphetamine, for instance, is a right-handed molecule. It is two to four times as stimulating to the brain as the left-handed, or levo methamphetamine molecule, the drug that is more commonly snorted, taken orally, or injected. However, this left-handed molecule is many times more stimulating to the cardiovascular system and nasal sinuses than the right-handed molecule. This is what makes an Ice high so different from the meth one typically snorts. But all of this had first to be discovered. In the early eighties it was, and by all the wrong people.

A few of these street chemists saw themselves through a kind of New Age prism, as Mother Nature's hierophant-scientists on a transcendent mission of developing mind-expanding drugs—or at least they were people with a mystical bent that believed in the aphorism "Better living through chemistry." But these folks were few and far between. Unlike those of marijuana and hallucinogenic drug cultures, these purveyors of altered states were overwhelmingly practical, having commercial objectives most squarely in mind. They were entrepreneurs interested in research and development of products they could sell. They knew R&D to be their lifeblood, the amphetamine molecule their clay, and they would always gather the wit to adapt to ever-changing laws, and the vagaries of the marketplace.

The supreme example of this remarkable blend of market savvy and technical ingenuity is still with us today, and has everything to do with the right-handed dextro isomer methamphetamine. In the late eighties legislation was passed that made ephedrine a controlled substance, just as P2P had become years earlier. Ephedrine could still be bought legally in Canada and Mexico, but had suddenly become difficult to come by in quantities required to fill the burgeoning demand chemists saw around them. This wouldn't be a problem for long, as the possibilities of a new precursor chemical were gradually being revealed in tiny labs scattered about the remote volcanic hills of Hawaii. Best of all, this new precursor was still legal.

The street chemists began to experiment with what was called pseudoephedrine, which just happens to be a left-handed molecule capable of forming a mirror image of itself, making a right-handed, dextro isomer methamphetamine base. From this Ice could be derived. It didn't take long for both the product and the knowledge (the recipe), to make its way to the mainland, for this is where the vast market lay. Thus by way of remarkable curiosity and cunning they opened up a whole new market. A problem—this one legal in nature—was translated into an asset, and fortunes multiplied. But this was only the early 1980s, and only one of many unsung achievements to come.

Over the course of the next two decades they would modify and simplify their techniques, making the process marginally safer (less combustible), and far more difficult to detect by developing a nearly odor-free method (the putrid smell associated with the manufacture of meth has often been the key to locating clandestine labs). In time methods would be developed so that the drugs could be made on a stovetop. Labs would be set up in mobile homes or ferried about in cars forever roaming the countryside, making interdiction all but impossible. The most difficult ingredients to come by, of course, would be ephedrine or pseudoephedrine. In time only a tiny percentage of labs would use P2P—roughly three percent today.

Not until the early 1980s would methamphetamine in its various forms fully regain its foothold in Europe and America. The epidemic that was to come would be far more devastating version than the one of mother's little helper and Black Beauties of the sixties, the White Crosses of the seventies. And the catastrophe didn't have to happen. Without the craven machinations of an inept U.S. Congress, and the innovations that allowed methamphetamine to be "home-made," the epidemic we live with today may never have been.

23

The bonfire smolders a thin grey soot within a ring of scattered bodies. Once the sun is up and shining on their sleeping figures, they gradually come to their feet, begin to stagger for their cars, hands absently pawing their pockets for car keys. Once again the ranch has lived up to its billing.

I've been awake through it all, the scene from the night before playing in my mind again and again. I doubt I'll ever see Lucille again, having, as she does, no reason to return. She has everything she thinks she'll ever need.

So at thirty-seven I am discarded in favor of a ranch hand and his newfangled moonshine. In the glare of first light the panic is still there. Then, as the morning advances, the feeling mutates into weird mixture of jealousy and rage, a mixture that obsesses the mind. Rage, it would seem, is the more liberating emotion, obsession's natural solvent.

Once everyone has left I head out to the shed Clyde said he had filled with hayseed. The door is still locked, so I go back for an axe used for last night's bonfire and begin hacking at the door. I have an idea of what I'm about to find, but nothing can quite prepare me for the bizarre reality.

The interior is aglitter. Everywhere, shelves and shelves of Pyrex glassware in the form of beakers, massive funnels, oversized test tubes, everything stained with a dull opaqueness. Propane tanks are stacked in a pyramid. It's all so weirdly neat yet filthy, like the laboratory lair of Dr. Frankenstein. And then the smell hits my sinuses: a scalding chemical stench, a distilled acidic pungency like that of a stagnant pool of cat urine. The air itself seems corrosive. With my shirt over my face, I shuffle over to Coleman cooler and lift the lid. Inside are quart-sized plastic containers labeled in block letters etched on rectangles of athletic tape: RED PHOSPHOUROUS, IODINE, PSEUDO-E, ACETONE, MURIATIC ACID, ACETONE, DENATURED ALCOHOL. Turning about, I see in the corner a tipi of automatic rifles and a stack of paper targets of human silhouettes. Alas I've seen enough.

By noon the sheriff's department has arrived in force—eight men with eight automatic rifles, side arms and body armor. After leading them to the shed a pot-bellied deputy with a thick black mustache pokes his head into the broken door, and then immediately orders everyone back to the house. With his head bobbing in familiar recognition, he says, "This isn't for us." His breath is labored as he walks beside me toward the house. "The county just got its own team for collecting evidence at meth labs, special criminologists who know this kind of thing." Apparently the ranch is now, in the deputy's words, "a hazardous crime scene." If this Clyde comes back, he points out, "he'll be armed to the teeth and pissed-*off.* I mean, these guys are *freaks* for violence, just cuckoo for Ko Ko Puffs."

Within the hour two new officers show up in a dated fire truck pulling a trailer marked "HAZARDOUS MATERIALS." It takes a full hour for them to dress in what they call their personal protection equipment, which includes a full-face air purifying respirator, a futuristic looking Tyvek suit, a pair of heavy chemical resistant gloves and oversized moon boots. We then lead them to the shed where they begin taking samples using an assortment of spatulas and pipettes. As we watch on, one of the suited officers turns to see us and then waves us away until we are a hundred yards or so from the shed. The potbellied sheriff's deputy hands me a pair of tiny binoculars.

"You're living next to a poison factory run by a psychopath," he says as I squint through the tiny lenses. "He mixes that red phosphorus with hydroiodic acid and it makes a phosphine gas. Couple of whiffs of that'll kill you."

"So you see this kind of thing a lot?" I ask.

"Oh, shit," he says breathlessly. "My brother-in-law got introduced my sister to meth. Now she's serving a fifteen-year sentence for shooting her neighbor's ten-year-old son with a deer rifle. It's everywhere." The first time he saw a lab, he goes on, his partner was blown up. A can of ethyl ether ignited the room when he flipped the light switch. The only time he's ever been shot at has been at the scene of a clandestine meth lab, and, as he says, "You never get used to that." So he's abundantly careful now, doesn't even mess with these labs anymore. He sees one, he calls in the forensic chemists, and they come in with plenty of heavily armed backup. Turning to me, he says with deadly seriousness, "I hate these people."

The deputy is familiar with the scene indeed. As I watch on through the binoculars, he keeps up a running commentary: "Now they're looking for any finished product…" A few seconds later, he continues on cue, "Next they'll put a silica gel desiccant on the rifles…" From time to time he takes the binoculars and seems to be instructing the forensic chemists telepathically. "All the documentary evidence goes in the clear kapak bags. Good job. Seal it and mark it. Contaminated evidence. Bingo." A few minutes later he says something that makes me feel suddenly weak: "Looks like they found one of those scrunchies women wear in their hair. They *love* these guys. The drugs make 'em skinny and super horny. So we have a barter system of goods for services."

Later in the day my father arrives to point out exactly where he found the chemical stash all those months ago. He's excited, his voice fluted with unspoken sorrow and apology. He won't say as much but he feels the terrible burden of having brought Clyde into the picture. I keep it light. "They'll find him," I say.

Moving about calms his inner strings. As we traverse the ranch there is a sense of dawning comprehension, a sense that we could find anything out here—scattered bones, a human skull with a hole in the temple. And as we move away from the shed the atmosphere becomes spooked. All that remains is something of a cave, a whorl of dried timothy hay that once encased so much evidence. Then comes a startled voice from across the way.

A detective at the edge of a far off pond is waving his hands. His delayed voice arcs over a dell, then his whistle pierces the distance. As we approach I see his eyes are tearing uncontrollably.

"I found the dump site," he says, palms in his eye sockets.

The rest of the afternoon is spent at the sheriff's office where we talk about the Aggies and prepare a statement. Who is Clyde's wife? I know her, I tell them. Could she be an accomplice? Not a chance. They're getting divorced. Someone asks for investment advice on various Internet stocks that aren't worth a shit. Eventually one of the forensic chemists approaches.

"Any girlfriends you know of?" he says.

I feel my face go hot.

"No idea."

"People don't just go out and do this by themselves. Not a big operation like this."

"I can't even speculate on Clyde's confederates," is all I can manage, and this would seem to be entirely satisfactory. Someone asks me where SunMicro will be in six months from now. "Down twenty." Half an hour later I'm back at the ranch.

That evening Colette's car appears in the drive. She steps out and stands within the arc of the opened door.

"I hear my story got some back-up," she says.

I approach the gate and lean my elbows on the orange surface rust.

"How'd you find out?"

"The cops showed up at the house a few hours ago."

"Imagine how surprised I am right now, Colette."

"What all didya learn?"

"The whole enchilada."

She closes her eyes very slowly and nods.

"So they're still looking for Clyde," she says.

"Where is he?"

"Somewhere out there," she says, indicating the world at large. "Rambling about with your wife."

Colette thoughtfully withdraws a cigarette from a Marlborough pack and offers me one. As we stand there smoking with the gate between us, she says, "You need to be careful. When Clyde finds out what happened to his operation, he's gonna be pretty steamed."

"Colette, I only hope he comes after me."

"You don't want that. He's smarter and meaner than he looks. He'll keep tabs on you—watch your house, watch you go to work, come back, figure out when you're not ready for him."

"And I'll keep tabs on him."

"Paranoid people are hard to sneak up on and they always seem to have a lot of time on their hands. They live in Crazy Town, and they have a way of pulling you in."

"Clyde might be mean," I say, "but he's not smart."

"He gets off on figuring things out for himself. He's too cheap to buy his own drugs, so he figures out how to make them. A few weeks ago he's in the yard tearing apart a bunch of lawn mowers, exchanging parts, trying to make one of them work...He'd love nothing better than to smash the brains out of whoever made off with his livelihood. And he'll do it while you're asleep."

"What a lovely thought, Colette."

She shrugs.

"It ain't lovely, Sterling, but it's your life."

24

Perhaps the street chemists' most enduring achievements have to do with the simplification and refinement of methods used to manufacture Ecstasy, or MDMA. Ecstasy was first developed in 1914 as an appetite suppressant, though rarely used as such. Sixty years later, in the 1970s, it was actually thought to be an effective aid in psychotherapy. Within a decade it would become the drug of choice among Ravers in England.

Ecstasy was popular there for a half-dozen years before wending its way through security at Florida airports in the mid-eighties. In South Florida it quickly became popular within the gay community in general and the dance clubs in particular. From there it made its way up the east coast, and then leap-frogged over the Heartland to California where it was immediately accepted and thought tremendously hip. Statistics confirm that the drug's popularity has hardly abated. In 1998 U.S. Customs officials confiscated a total of 750,000 doses of Ecstasy. The following year they seized three million. In 2000 the total exceeded six million—and these are only among the drugs that smugglers attempt to bring in from abroad, and that were subsequently confiscated. A shocking reality lay just under the surface like an iceberg. By then Ecstasy, like methamphetamine, was easily and widely manufactured in domestic clandestine labs, and this is the source of the overwhelming majority of the Ecstasy used today. Surely one of Ecstasy's greatest assets is the fact that young people are among its most ardent fans, a seemingly built-in trait that keeps it perennially popular. A recent federally sponsored survey of high school students indicated that Ecstasy use among high school seniors had increased fifty-five percent in the twelve months from 1998 to 1999.

It's recent history is peculiar indeed, and bespeaks the mercurial nature of the amphetamine molecule. Because Ecstasy's molecular structure is slightly different from that of methamphetamine, the drug wasn't technically illegal in the United States until 1985. The altered molecular structure of course produces a different psychological (as well as legal, if found in possession only a few years ago) effect on the user, one quite different than methamphetamine. MDMA works by act-ing on the seratonin receptor sites in the brain, enabling them to take in large amounts of seratonin, and other neurotransmitters, namely dopamine. Seratonin's role is remarkably broad in scope. This is the chemical the brain employs to govern sleep, complex learning processes, and the integration of emotion. As would be expected, heavy use of Ecstasy causes the brain to produce less seratonin, which typically results in long-term depression and general anxiety when the user attempts to quit.

In recent years a peculiar debate has sprung up regarding the dangers inherent to the drug. During the 1970s a tiny corner of the psychiatric community believed small doses of MDMA (forty to sixty milligrams) to be safe and effective in treating depression. Some therapists actually took the drugs themselves, as they thought it helped them connect to and empathize with their patients, which, they argued, made them more effective therapists. Yet evidence of Ecstasy's neurotoxicity is indisputable. The drug has been shown to produce hydrogen peroxide as the seratonin receptors attempt to break down dopamine. This hydrogen peroxide, researchers at NIDA believe, causes long-term damage to the neurons in the brain that transmit seratonin. Because of its questionable medicinal value, MDMA was placed on Schedule I of the CSA.

The deaths that are blamed on Ecstasy use, however, are not a direct result of the drug's meddling with brain chemistry. More often than not, death is a result of dehydration that comes from dancing for hours on end without rest. Of course Ecstasy is ultimately the cause, as it suppresses thirst and the need for sleep, while it compels users into repetitive motion—very much like its sister drug, methamphetamine. Dozens of deaths annually, however, have been attributed to a user overcompensating with water, and actually becoming overhydrated, which can also be fatal. A great many of those who have died do so on a crowded dance floor surrounded by strangers, whirling lights, and the mindless throb of techno-pop, all the while in the grip of a seizure escorts them into the next world.

Methamphetamine would seem to be a most malleable clay. Indeed, one does not need to toy with its molecule much in order to drastically alter its effect on the user. The drug MDA (2-methylenedioxyamphetamine), for example, looks a lot like MDMA at the molecular level. Subtle differences in structure, however, make it more hallucinogenic than MDMA. In moderate doses, MDA produces effects much like that of LSD, while at higher doses the user behaves more like someone on high doses of amphetamine. The effect is similar enough that on the street it is still known as Ecstasy.

The history of MDA parallels that of amphetamine to a remarkable degree. MDA was first synthesized in Germany in 1910, and was later thought to have medicinal value in the treatment of Parkinson's disease, and as an antidepressant. The pharmaceutical company of Smith, Klein and French saw potential in MDA as an appetite suppressant (as many companies recognized amphetamine), and sold it for a time under the trade name Amphedoxamine. At the height of the Cold War the U.S. military thought it might prove useful as a truth serum, a kind of hallucinogenic sodium pentothal. Like all such substances with a recreational potential, it was discovered by the infinitely curious counterculture of the sixties. Once discovered, it would never be forgotten. Today it is sold illicitly in tablet form, and is one of the most popular designer drugs on the street.

Another amphetamine analogue is MDE, or 3,4-methylenedioxyethamphetamine. Known on the street as "Eve," MDE's effects are said to be very similar to those of MDA. Anecdotal accounts among users suggest that it's generally less potent and the effects shorter in duration (two or three hours). They tend to report a less hallucinogenic effect than MDA, with many claiming MDE made them feel merely drunk or stoned. Like Ecstasy, a dozen or so users die every year as a result from taking the drug. Similarly, the cause of death is typically hyperthermia.

Yet another analogue drug is a kind of crossbreed between methamphetamine and cathinone, called methcathinone. On the street it's simply "Cat," or sometimes "Star." Cat is so new that it wasn't strictly illegal in the United States until 1993 when it was placed on Schedule I of the CSA. The cathinone is derived from the Catha edulis shrub, a plant indigenous to east Africa and the Arabian Peninsula. For centuries people there have chewed the young leaves of the plant for its stimulant properties. Methcathinone, however, is a far more powerful hybrid, a blending of the ancient and modern methods of pharmacology. Cat is far more potent than its parent drug, and today is produced almost exclusively in clandestine labs that use ephedrine as its base. Like methamphetamine, Cat incites the brain's neurotransmitters norepinephrine and dopamine to produce the same general sense of euphoria and well-being. It was first synthesized in 1928 and went on to be used as an antidepressant and appetite suppressant. Like meth, it increases the user's energy and also inspires some remarkably erratic and violent behavior.

For reasons that are not entirely clear, the various amphetamine analogues are not equally toxic. Methamphetamine, for instance, appears to be far more detrimental than, say, Ecstasy. The longstanding conventional wisdom concerning the neurotoxicity of meth was that the drug damages but does not kill nerve cells in the brain. Research conducted on animals at NIDA indicates that damage occurred primarily to nerve endings of brain cells containing dopamine. Once exposure to methamphetamine stopped, the nerve endings were believed to recover, at least partially, within a few months. That is, the dopamine levels gradually came back, and brain function was more or less normal. Recent brain imaging studies on human beings, however, show a different picture.

Dr. Jean Lud Cadet, clinical director of Intramural Research Program of the National Institute on Drug Abuse, has conducted ground-breaking research on the damage caused by heavy methamphetamine use. The conclusions he and his team arrived at go far beyond what was once conventional wisdom.

"People used to think that the most serious methamphetamine-induced damage was to dopamine nerve terminals because it put people at risk for developing Parkinson's disease as they got older," Dr. Cadet says. "It does not just destroy the endings of dopamine-containing nerve cells. It also kills other nerve cells that produce other neurotransmitters in additional brain pathways."[1]

The damage inflicted on the brain is also believed to last longer than previous thought—for at least three years after the addict stops using. In some ways, the brain never recovers. Cadet's research indicates that methamphetamine triggers a natural mechanism called *apoptosis*, which prompts widespread cell death in the striatum, hippocampus, and frontal cortex regions of the brain. Perhaps the most alarming aspect of this research has to do with the fact that these areas were previously believed to be untouched by heavy methamphetamine use. This is frightening for a very real reason. The damage appears to induce alterations in brain chemistry in long-term methamphetamine users similar to that found in people suffering from stroke or Alzheimer's disease. The leading theory puts forth that by killing the nerve cells that produce other neurotransmitters, meth in effect chokes off the free electrical commerce of the brain.

On the face of it, premature onset of Alzheimer's symptoms seems an ironic fate for the methamphetamine addict. The hyper-life they once pursued delivers them to a vacant and mindless world of premature elderliness. They all come to share an array of traits that lend an appearance of the failing senior citizen: the skullish eyes, the shedding of teeth, decaying fingernails, and ceaseless tremor running through the limbs—and all of it self-inflicted. The source is a lightning bolt that has made its way through their lives, searing the tender membranes through which they once apprehended a more subtle, complex and beautiful world.

---

1. Ironically, Hitler's Dr. Morrell treated his most notorious patient with a drug that is now thought not only to aggravate but to precipitate the very disease he was trying to treat.

25

I'm laid up with the flu on the sofa in the upstairs office of my empty new house, a quilt draped over my legs. The fever broke around noon and now the chills are slowly ebbing. I'm watching the Rangers lose in extra innings of the 2000 season home opener when I fall asleep. Then the phone rings. The clock reads 12:20 A.M. The caller I.D. reads HOUSTON P.D. After a foggy initial exchange, a Houston paramedic asks if I know a woman by the name of Lucille.

The sense of déjà vu is caught up in my vague, fluish dreams. As I slowly come-to, the first impulse is to instruct the paramedic to send Lucille home, for her husband needs her back. Heartsickness has translated into longstanding physical illness. Then the anger arrives, surprisingly close at hand.

"The last time I saw her," I groan, "she was bent over a lavatory with a pile of meth in her face and a hyena on her tail."

The puzzled voice turns adamant and stern. He would appreciate it if I would come extract my estranged wife from a rather fantastic situation.

"What's the situation?" I inquire.

"Four hours ago the police found her walking down the middle of a street here in Rice Village. Stuttering and seeing snakes and UFOs everywhere. Obviously tweaking. Wouldn't give her name, didn't have a purse or I.D. A few minutes ago she jotted down her name and this number."

"Where is she now?"

"The E.R. at Ben Taub."

"Can I talk to her?"

"You can talk to her all you want when you get here."

The hospital hallways are crowded with the sick and dying among Houston's indigent huddled masses. Gunshot wounds, drug overdoses, a diabetic rummy with a gangrenous foot lie on the floor and on gurneys. Deep within the hospital's lighted caverns I find Lucille sitting in a chair looking like a duck that's been struck on the head. Perhaps it's a distortion of my fluish brain, but her attenuated neck seems impossibly long, her eyes skullishly round and wide. Every small sound draws her attention; her head reacts in panicked jerks. The moment she sees me she appears outraged, betrayed by the strangers who brought her here.

"What happened, Lucille?" I say as I approach.

"I was drugged," she whispers. "Somebody drugged me."

"Hope one of these cops doesn't find out you've violated the conditions of your probation."

She says nothing; merely stares, crazy as a loon. When I finally unlock my eyes from hers, I see a doctor hurriedly approaching.

"We have twenty-four hours to do the swab test," he says, not bothering to introduce himself.

"What's the swab test for?" I ask.

"Collection of DNA."

"For a drug overdose?"

He turns to Lucille confidentially.

"We can either do it now or you can come back in the morning."

I turn to Lucille.

"What's he talking about?"

Lucille shrugs.

"Were you drugged or what?" I ask.

I follow her roving eyes as a cop walks by the foot of the bed. She says nothing. Even in her deluded state Lucille knows it's better not to commit to any specific story.

"You need to make a decision about the test by morning," the doctor says.

"Would it be all right if we stepped outside for a cigarette?" I ask.

"Just see that you talk to me before you go."

With that he walks off to his next case, disappearing into the crowd.

I take a step back from Lucille, watch her as she sits all alone on this gurney in the midst of this hospital bustle. A few hours ago, I remind myself, she was seeing snakes, and now she's shrewdly plotting diversionary tactics. In an emancipating moment of clarity she saw a way to make the police officers go away, to have them replaced by hospital staff. It's all quite simple. Instead of the abuser, she would become the abused.

"S-somebody at a party put something in my drink," she says as another cop walks by. "Can we sort this out at home?"

"You moved out, so to speak, two weeks ago."

"Just take me home."

I reach for her clipboard hanging from the bedstead, yank away the case sheet, and together we weave through the maze of doctors and nurses, patients and cops. As we come out into the cold evening air, I say, "So where have you been?"

She mumbles something. When I press her for an answer, she instructs me to be quiet; she is scanning the night skies for microwave signals of extraterrestrial origin. We climb into the car I came in, and then head into the heart of Rice Village in the vicinity of the neighborhood that Lucille left the Jaguar. After cruising the streets for an hour, we come upon a dark shape pulled high up onto the curb. I step out and see the keys are in the ignition, Lucille's purse on the floor. The car and everything in it is just as she abandoned it hours earlier.

I pull the car off the curb, park it, grab Lucille's purse and lock everything up. When I come back Lucille's eyes are open, but her head gently bobs against the seatbelt harness as though she were asleep.

"You need to get back into rehab," I say, tossing her purse into her lap. Seeing it, she instantly plunges a hand into the cluster of effects. A moment later she produces a tremendous baggie, an inch or so deep, of crystal. I snatch it from her, lower my window, and toss it.

She slowly turns to look me in the eyes.

"I do not know who you are," she says mystically.

"I'm the guy who put Clyde out of business."

"Clyde," she mutters to herself, again and again. In time "Clyde" becomes "Co-llide."

"You're in Crazy Town, Lucille."

She freezes. "Who told you about Crazy Town?"

"Colette, your boyfriend's wife."

Her eyes slowly grow wide. In her world Crazy Town is really a place, and I am an interloper who is not to be trusted.

And so I learn to recognize patterns as they emerge from the chaos. Spaceships hover in the near darkness. Cops supplant the threat of snakes. She was drugged, she was raped. Hence, reality is discernable to Lucille but hangs impaled upon the hallucination. In her current state of mind reality is an infinitely malleable thing. Such insanity used to make sense only to Lucille. Now it makes sense to me.

When we arrive at the house Lucille has to be coaxed out of the car, as she thinks the driveway has turned into grape Jello. If she steps on it she will sink and drown. I don't try very hard to get her inside, and that seems to convince her all is safe. Of her own wit and volition she points out that I am not sinking. "A sound observation," I remark.

Inside I set her down before the television where she sits erect studying a Tom and Jerry episode on Cartoon Network. Within minutes she's asleep. She stays asleep through what remains of the night. In the morning I'm well enough to go to work, but when I come home she's still unconscious. And then comes the mystery. Sometime deep in the night, long after I'm lost in sleep, I sense a shift in my dreams—like a buckle in a summer breeze that portends the approach of weather. A warm pressure descends and enters the world of indistinct dreams but tugs at that outer world. The mist of illusion fades, and Lucille becomes present, her hair tumbling down over my head. *I need you*, she whispers. Release follows an exquisite moment of tension. Her weight lifts from the bed, and slips away like a spectral form.

In the morning Lucille lies burrowed face down in a fetal position on the sofa, just as I'd initially left her two nights ago. When I return in the evening she is again asleep, although there is evidence that she's been awake. That night as I lie in bed I hear her moving about the kitchen. The refrigerator crushes some ice, a toilet flushes. The microwave beeps. I come downstairs, only to find her again asleep. Never awake. A rectangle of macaroni and cheese teeters on the edge of the coffee table. As I step out of the shower at dawn the next morning I hear her on the phone. A few seconds later the backdoor opens and closes. From the upstairs window I see her walking down the sidewalk, her mop of black hair blowing in the light breeze. Clyde's pickup pulls alongside the curb. She gets in and away she goes in a violent roar.

Later that morning I see a sticky note on the kitchen counter marked in Lucille's swooping schoolgirl script. Perhaps a word on where I can reach her. Goodbye, maybe. On it are scrawled three lines: "Feeling better now. Thanks for being there, xo L."

So Lucille becomes a ghost in my life. For a full six weeks I neither see nor hear from her, and I come to wonder whether or not the last strange night ever happened at all. And then that suddenly changes when I come home from work one evening that spring.

I don't notice it at first. Fifteen solid hours of arcane problem solving have numbed my brain. But as I sit in the silence of the living room, staring straight ahead at the kitchen, I see a bright square note against the dark cherry wood of the cabinet, and recognize at once that Lucille has been here. I thrust myself to my feet and come into the kitchen. But it takes a moment in my present state to apprehend the full gravity of what the note says. And yet it is quite simple. "Think I might be pregnant, L."

26

In 1985 an analogue drug-related arrest meant nothing. It might as well have never happened. A trip to the crime lab produced the extraordinary result of an exculpatory analysis, which was inevitably followed by a get-out-of-jail-free card for user, dealer, and manufacturer alike. The following year everything changed. Congress passed the Drug Analogue and Anti-Drug Abuse Acts, which expressly forbade all possible variations of controlled substances—even those that had yet to be discovered.

Before the legislation designer drugs had three reasons for being: They were relatively easy to make, fun to take, and they were legal. In 1986 the third reason was suddenly and permanently scratched off the list, but this wasn't enough to make the drugs go away. They were still easy to make and fun to take. Indeed, they were becoming all the more easy to make, and refined methods arguably made them all the more pleasurable.

But the methamphetamine phenomenon has always been about producing drugs with equipment and chemicals that are widely available to the general public. Of course there are drugs other than those of the amphetamine family made by street chemists (namely LSD and White China, a synthetic heroin), but the reality is that the overwhelming majority of lab seizures are of those making methamphetamine. According to DEA numbers, currently well over eighty percent of clandestine lab seizures are meth labs.

The key to the phenomenon is the ubiquitous and otherwise benign nature of the chemicals used—P2P, ephedrine and pseudoephedrine in particular. The street chemist's Achilles heel has been, only until very recently, their ability to acquire these precursor chemicals in ample quantities. By the late 1980s, bulk ephedrine powder became the raw material of choice, as the hydriodic acid/ephedrine reduction method was widely understood to be a simple, high-yielding method of producing methamphetamine.

But in 1988 the legal landscape again shifted with an amendment to the CSA that included the Chemical Diversion and Trafficking Act (CDTA). The CDTA required importers and exporters of controlled substances, namely bulk ephedrine and P2P to keep records and notify federal authorities of the comings and goings of their products. However, companies who manufacture legitimate over-the-counter products containing ephedrine lobbied with all their might to keep their ephedrine-based products exempt from the CDTA. Cold medicine, which comes in tablet and capsule form, they argued, could be legally marketed and distributed under the Food, Drug and Cosmetic Act. After much haggling among lawmakers, lobbyists, and activists, an accommodation was reached on behalf of the pharmaceutical companies. In the CDTA's final draft, an exemption was provided for tablets and capsules containing ephedrine, allowing them to remain largely unregulated. The drug companies had prevailed. So too had the street chemists.

It was a classic legislative loophole. Street chemists understood that tablets and capsules could just as easily be purchased and converted into methamphetamine as powder procurers, and a huge new market opened up for people who could supply them with sufficient quantities. According to DEA estimates, it takes approximately 48,000 twenty-five-milligram tablets to extract a single kilogram of pure ephedrine or pseudoephedrine. From this kilo the street chemist can expect to harvest anywhere from fifty to seventy-five percent of this weight in useable methamphetamine.

Buyers and sellers would get together in the most public of forums. These uncontrolled ephedrine tablets could be easily purchased in the quantities required from mail order distributors who brazenly marketed ephedrine tablets in one-hundred and one-thousand-count bottles in ads in national magazines such as Cosmopolitan, High Times, and Hustler. When confronted by law enforcement, these mail-order outfits claimed to be selling these colossal supplies of ephedrine and pseudoephedrine tablets as energy boosters, weight-loss supplements and bronchodilators. Denial of any criminal intent or knowledge of what these supplies were being used for was a matter of course. Prosecutors everywhere recognized that even the most egregious abuses were difficult to take on in a court of law due to the exemption provided for in the current legislation.

In response, the Department of Justice's Office of Diversion Control drafted the Domestic Chemical Diversion Control Act (DCDCA) in 1990. The proposed legislation sought to close the ephedrine tablet and capsule loophole and give law enforcement the authority to go after companies diverting large quantities of precursor chemicals without proving that they had criminal intent. In 1993 the law finally passed Congress and became effective the following spring. Incredibly, the legislation only removed the exemption for over-the-counter ephedrine tablets, but not for pseudoephedrine products—again, the result of a furious lobbying effort on the part of the cold medicine industry. The effect on the methamphetamine trade was hydraulic in nature: chemists simply shifted from ephedrine to pseudoephedrine, making the more potent d-methamphetamine instead of the less potent l-methamphetamine. Such conflicted legislation could be said to have garnered a net loss in the never-ending war on drugs.

Three years later came yet more legislation, with the Methamphetamine Control Act of 1996 (MCA). These new laws brought controls on drug products containing ephedrine, pseudoephedrine, and P2P, and broadened the list of controlled chemicals known to be used by clandestine lab operators. And this is how blister packs for cold medicines came into being—a so-called "safe harbor" exemption demanded by the over-the-counter pharmaceutical industry. The theory they put forward to Congress was that the nuisance of blister packs would be a significant deterrent at the retail level for the meth cook. According to Rogene Waite of the DEA's Office of Diversion, the "DEA did not accept this theory." And for good reason. Sitting around the house and peeling foil from thousands of blister packs is just the kind of repetitive motion meth users are drawn to. In October of 2001 the DEA recommended to Congress that they remove the blister pack exemption.

The sheer scale of some of these clandestine precursor diversion operations was staggering. In 1995 the DEA became suspicious of a company located in western Pennsylvania by the name of Clifton Pharmaceuticals. Import/export declarations being filed by a number of bulk importers of ephedrine and pseudoephedrine powder revealed that huge quantities were being brought into the United States, and an ensuing investigation indicated that Clifton Pharmaceuticals was one of their principle customers. Clifton had customers of its own, which turned out to be three mail-order firms based in Florida and Kentucky. All the while, their chemicals had been turning up in clandestine labs that had been seized all over the western United States.

In May of 1995 undercover DEA agents approached Clifton Pharmaceuticals and purchased twenty-million sixty-milligram pseudoephedrine tablets for $180,000. The sale triggered the execution of a federal search and seizure warrant at the Clifton plant, where they came across enough ephedrine, pseudoephedrine, and P2P powder, tablets and capsules to fill five fifty-foot tractor trailers. The ephedrine and pseudoephedrine alone weighed twenty-five metric tons.

Meanwhile the methamphetamine trade continued to evolve in the wake of every piece of new federal legislation passed. After passage of the CDTA, U.S. and Mexican border patrols noted a spike in the amount of precursor chemicals being confiscated along the familiar drug routes between the two countries. Instead of manufacturing methamphetamine in Mexico where they could do so with impunity, they clearly preferred completing the process in the United States.

The reason had everything to do with drug laws and the nature of the methamphetamine molecule. Smuggling methamphetamine itself could now bring serious prison time. Getting busted for cold medicine—even in large quantities and with obvious criminal intent—was an entirely different matter. But that is the mission statement of designer drugs: They are designed to get around laws.

The chemicals were typically carried by poor Mexican immigrants by way of established drug smuggling routes to large-scale labs in remote locales scattered throughout the hills of California. To their experience, the money was good and the risk slight, even if they were apprehended by U.S. authorities. Penalties added up to little more than deportation. In the eyes of the law these suspects weren't smuggling kilos of actual meth, but mere cold medicine.

In this way risk was minimized while profits rivaled that of cocaine and heroine smuggling. Of course there is no way of smuggling opiates in their component parts, which only enhanced meth's allure among the conventional Mexican drug cartels. According to DEA figures, an investment in chemicals of five-hundred dollars will yield about a pound of methamphetamine. One pound of meth sells for a little less than twenty-thousand dollars—nearly a forty-fold return on one's investment. In time Mexican traffickers would become the dominant force in the American meth manufacturing trade.

But even the Mexican cartels had to get their ephedrine, pseudoephedrine or P2P from somewhere, and getting adequate quantities through customs wouldn't always go flawlessly. In March of 1994 U.S. Customs Service at Dallas/Fort Worth Airport came across a peculiar shipment that had originated in Zurich, Switzerland on its way to Mexico City. The only reason it caught the attention of Customs officials was because they discovered that the shipment lacked the proper export documentation. Upon closer examination they saw that the cardboard drums had had their labeling removed, and that the lids had been turned inside out. The broker's name had also been concealed with black paint. Upon opening the drums, they found 3.4 metric tons of ephedrine.

The ephedrine had been manufactured by a company in India, and then brokered by a firm in Zurich who in turn shipped it to Mexico. However, because of scheduling difficulties, the flight was diverted to Dallas/Fort Worth Airport where it came under U.S. jurisdiction. At the time it was the largest shipment ever intercepted by American law enforcement since the passage of the CDTA, and it was purely by accident that it was discovered. The unlikely seizure could only be interpreted as the visible portion of a very extensive problem, the tip of a very large iceberg.

The discovery spurred a flurry of investigations, which eventually revealed a pattern in the international chemical diversion trade. Huge amounts of precursor chemicals were being produced in, of all places, the Czech Republic, and then sent to Switzerland. There one of three Swiss firms sent the chemicals on their way to a Mexico. In one year in the mid-1990s, Swiss officials acknowledged that at least seventy metric tons had been shipped. Mexican cartels had developed other supply channels, which originated in India and China, transiting through the United Arab Emirates, Holland, and Guatemala. In short, Mexican labs and obscure clandestine labs all across America had an unlimited supply of precursor chemicals, and by the mid-1990s, the United States was flooded with meth. Precursors and the labs that processed them were everywhere. And so was the once-most-elusive ingredient—the knowledge. The medium for the knowledge was altogether new, something that delivered information freely and ubiquitously.

Crazy Town

27

Colette sits on the porch swing, gently tossing herself back and forth with a little kick of the pointed toes of her lace-up boots. Her eyes are lost in the distance, the black shape of bats darting about as they scour the night sky.

"Lucille's with child," I hear myself say. "Eight weeks along."

Colette turns to me and smiles. "That'll be Clyde's fifth," she remarks with utter nonchalance.

"It could be mine."

Her eyes wander as she calculates weeks and timelines.

"So you've had a visitor."

I nod. "Wasn't my finest hour."

"Men are weak."

We both fall silent as the sound of insects fills the air, the soft cringing of the porch swing's rusty chains. Then Colette suddenly laughs.

"Not too long ago I saw your trouble first-hand," she says with kindly, knowing condescension.

"You'll have to be more specific."

"Clyde and Lucille. Doing what they do best. I saw it all."

"What did you see?"

In so many words Colette characterizes the story as everything I "didn't want to know." Within it lay the mystery of Clyde's and Lucille's biochemical attraction, the mad science that drew them together, all of the elements that made this sordid affair possible.

"It was weird, like the both of them didn't even know or care that I was there watching what they were doing."

"Why do you suppose they didn't care?"

"Clyde was making a statement: 'This is my new life, Colette. This is my new job, this is my new woman.'"

◆　　◆　　◆

There had been divorce papers to be signed, so Colette stopped by the ranch that night looking for Clyde, as he hadn't been home yet. The lights to my ranch house were off, but there was a flicker out in the adjacent hay pastures. She walked out where she found Lucille and Clyde kneeling among what she initially took for garage clutter at the edge of the moonlit clearing near the shed. Lucille was kneeling in the soft earth as she held an oversized test-tube in the beam of a miner's lamp strapped to Clyde's head. Their hands, encased in cream-colored latex gloves, glowed in the weird light as Clyde directed a jet of engine starter fluid through the aperture of the test-tube. Seeing Colette approach, Clyde simply said, "Lucille, this is my soon-to-be ex-wife, Colette."

"I'd shake your hand right now," Lucille said sweetly, like a happy homemaker, "but my hands are kinda full."

With her hands on her hips, Colette shouted, *"Clyde, what in the hell are you doing?"*

Clyde momentarily paused, deeply annoyed that she couldn't see for herself the self-evident nature of the scene before her.

"You have papers at home to sign," she added.

"Hold your goddamn horses till I'm done," he shot back, "and I'll sign whatever you want." He didn't ask her to leave. So she stood there, watching and waiting, unaware of just how long it would be, and amazed at her husband's ingenuity. His is an *organized* mind, she told herself, but also a *criminal* mind…

It's a fairly straight-forward process with which I am now familiar, and therefore easy to visualize through Colette's narrative. For the next few hours Clyde conveyed to his new girlfriend all the small secrets, the methods that separated the good stuff from the great. Clyde relentlessly pressed Lucille with the hard sell. He knew it all—four or five syntheses, designed to allow for the ingredients on hand—and he was willing to take her on as his pupil. Lucille was all smiles.

First he poured tap water from a canteen into the test-tube, and then brought a vulcanized thumb over the top and began to shake it for what seemed a ridiculously long time, as though he was going on and on like this for show, evidence of a steely work ethic. Once done he took an eyedropper and drew off the milky ether that had risen to the top like cream and squirted it into a beaker. Next, he took a pale brick of driveway cleaner and carved off a couple of ounces into another beaker that held the cottons from dozens of Vick's inhalers. He then added a third of an ounce of water and kneaded the concoction together, gradually wringing a noxious liquid from the cotton. This he poured through a coffee filter and into yet another beaker, producing a smell so sharp, so pungent of cat urine, it made everyone involuntarily gag. Colette herself was sent into the surrounding darkness for a breath of fresh air. Standing upright, she recalls seeing the approach of a thunderstorm on the horizon, the soft lateral flashes of a monsoon floating up from the Gulf, momentarily losing herself in the strange beauty of the view.

When she came back Lucille was kneeling beside Clyde who was stirring a solution of lye crystals in the form of Drano that had been mixed with the original broth. He then mixed in the ether. After a few minutes of shaking, the ether rose to the top of the batter, and again he drew it off the top with the eyedropper. Finally, Clyde made a separate solution of hydrochloric acid and water, and added it to the broth. All was then poured into a Pyrex dish that sat upon the soft blue ring of a liquid-propane stove. Clyde carefully monitored and adjusted the flame as crystals slowly formed at the edges of shallow lagoons, crystals he recognized in a thrilling moment as pure methamphetamine hydrochloride. He tapped his temple and said, "It's all right up here."

Meanwhile, the broth continued to boil off and crystallize. In the final evaporative moment, Lucille began shaking her smiling head. The final pool thickened as the storm approached. Clyde scraped away the warm crystals with a razor blade, and then scooped them into a Zip-lock freezer bag. The gentle rumble of thunder could now be heard in the near-distance as a massive storm cell was suddenly charged.

Suspended in the beam of his miner's lamp, cradled in the clear bag, was three-thousand dollars, Clyde said. To make more, all he said he needed were a few hundred Vick's inhalers, but what he had his eye on was a new synthesis out of Phoenix using pseudoephedrine capsules—"the good shit." That was what his life had become anymore, Colette recalled: Clyde sitting before the blue glow of the TV screen in their living room, tearing away the foil from thousands of blister packs of cold medicine while he watched the Road Runner and Wile E. Coyote wage war. This was his great problem, the one he complained to Lucille about now. Everywhere he went, every foray into a neighboring county, he made of point of passing through the local Wal-Mart, CostCo, Walgreens, whatever, to pick up three packs of inhalers or capsules. But the pharmacists, standing there like cigar store Indians, knew what he was up to, always had that knowing suspicion in their stare that turned to naked contempt as he approached the counter. His big plan was to one day drive to Mexico where you could buy psuedoephedrine tablets by the dry-wall-bucket full. No more blister packs, no more bitchy pharmacists. But now, as they sat in this field, it was a moment of celebration.

Clyde hauled all of his materials and equipment back to a shed, and then announced, "It's Miller Time!" Colette recalls Lucille wanting to carry the bag as they walked toward the house. Clyde happily surrendered it, all buck-teeth and grins. Colette followed, although both Clyde and Lucille now seemed entirely unaware of her presence, both having but one thing on their mind. When they came inside Clyde headed directly to the bathroom and reappeared with a framed picture. He and Lucille then settled into the sofa as Clyde picked out a marble-sized rock and began shaving it against the picture glass, forming a soft yellow powder that seemed to melt under his razor blade. "Here's your ticket to Crazy Town," he murmured. He then drew a half-dozen lines which they snorted through a tightly rolled five-dollar bill. The same bill had been used so much in this capacity that Lincoln's face was polished smooth and appeared glazed with perspiration.

Momentarily Lucille was off by herself in the corner by the big-screen TV with her hands in the air, hips slowly gyrating, dancing to music that existed only within the auditorium of her mind. Across the room Clyde strutted like a rooster, back and forth before the sofa and coffee table. He was the man. In his crystalline dream he was no longer the bonehead with dirt under his fingernails whose ambitions never seem to materialize, who has only known approval from people who don't know him very well. Not now as he strutted about the room, his tiny chin jutting, his mind racing with vague thoughts of personal glory. He was the hero-chemist, the chef who knew how to make some kick-ass speed and now his employer's sexy wife's knight in shining armor. He would be this person for the next three or four sleepless days, and then, when the human aliens arrive in their invisible spaceship, he would become someone very different.

All the while Lucille danced away in the corner. Clyde came right up to her, eyes and then hands molding the enhanced sway of her torso. Colette says she was way beyond caring, and has been for a long time now.

The night would have gone on and on like this, but suddenly Clyde was shouting that he saw headlights coming up the road leading to the ranch. Within a matter of seconds the picture was back on the bathroom wall and the meth in its baggie. Clyde then lunged for Lucille's elbow and guided her to the backdoor.

Colette followed them as they ran toward the woods. Clyde claimed he could hear the radios in the police car, the voices of the cops peering through the windows. Then they were gone, lost in the wet and swarming undergrowth, holding hands as they ran, utterly convinced they were now on the lam.

Then Colette headed back to the house where she found no police.

"You know whose car it was that pulled up?" Colette now says.

"No idea."

"Our seventeen-year-old son's. Out looking for his daddy. Wondered if he needed a ride home from work because he knows his truck doesn't always start in the rain. Try explaining all of that to a kid."

The cringe of the rusty porch swing chains suddenly seem so loud.

"What did you tell him?" I ask.

"That his daddy was chasing drug peddlers off Mr. Braswell's property."

"Chasing himself."

"In the tiniest circle."

28

The World Wide Web has been described as an "ethereal wilderness," inhabited as it is by eccentrics and madmen roving about everyday society and commerce. Exotic pockets coexist alongside the most sober and commonplace sites with a harmony that simply doesn't occur outside cyberspace. It's the perfect stage for the outrageous. The most provocative sites are surely the free-for-all forums that would seem to be hell-bent on testing the limits of free speech in a liberal democracy.

One of the most audacious is one of its most peculiar. It goes by the name Temple of the Screaming Electron, or totse.com. Here one finds opinion, facts, myth, stories and stark, raw data. Some of the information, it would seem, goes well beyond the pale of legality. There's an abundance of information, including recipes, on how to manufacture various kinds of methamphetamine.

Totse.com is the brainchild of two men by the name of Jeff Hunter and J.C. Stanton. It initially came into being in 1989 as a dial-up system run on a computer with a tiny 20 megabyte hard drive, and gradually evolved into a web-based system running on ten servers with multiple phone lines and high-speed modems. Its literature claims to have once had the largest text file repository in the world as of 1997. According to Stanton, the traffic it sees today is astounding: 89,000 hits per hour, 38,000,000 during the month of February 2003 alone.

On the surface, co-administrator J.C. Stanton seems to be an intensely private person. He is, but of necessity. He's wary of granting interviews, and is emphatic that he knows very little about methamphetamine. He has never made it, thinks it a horrible drug. If he grants an interview, he'll call you from a pay phone at an agreed-upon time. His sense of privacy, however, doesn't stem from a fear of the law.

"If law enforcement wanted to know who I am," he says, "they could get a subpoena in ten minutes. It wouldn't be a problem for them." His sense of privacy is a result of the fact that "we get a lot of mail from crazy people, and I don't want them to know who I am."

A cursory glance at the Temple of the Screaming Electron, and his point becomes clear. A column of icons running down the left side of the first page has headings such as COMMUNITY, BAD IDEAS, DRUGS, EGO, EROTICA,

FRINGE, SOCIETY, TECHNOLOGY. BAD IDEAS has pieces entitled "Guns and Weapons," and "Irresponsible Activities," which has the tagline, "How to be a real pain in the ass." Another piece entitled "KA-FUCKING-BOOM!" announces that it is about bombs, rockets and things that go BOOM! It informs visitors of ten high explosive mixtures they can make at home. Another piece is entitled "An Aussie Beer Can Mortar." In it a fellow with a military background who calls himself Andy tells us the story of how he made such a mortar—and how you can too!

Pages found under the DRUGS icon are of a similar shrill bent. Those intended as manuals for synthesizing controlled substances are typically conveyed in the first person by a very high-strung narrative voice. Others concern methods of subverting drug tests, how to cook with pot, how to have fun with nutmeg, how to purify heroin, how to make the drug Special K from liquid ketamine, how to make MDMA from Eugenol. One article by a man who goes by "Freddy Fender" offers the most trenchant and chilling advice: "In the west, California in particular, the meth market is monopolized by 'bikers' and anyone producing meth without their knowledge is risking quite a bit of wrath…anyone SELLING meth independently is risking death. So the advice is: If you make meth, tell the bikers." Mr. Fender then goes on to announce the good news for chemists. "Ninety-nine percent of all narcotics lab-busting is geared toward meth and other amphetamines. Labs that produce psychedelics are safer than ever."

Stanton's site is both a nexus and a sounding board for a gathering of voices heard almost no where else on the planet. Although Stanton himself claims never to have engaged in making methamphetamine or any kind of homemade drug, he seems to have his finger on the pulse of the scene. He lives in an undisclosed metropolitan area where, he says, "methamphetamine has become primarily a gay party drug," a role it has taken on nationwide. His best insights, however, concern the phenomenon of clandestine manufacturing. "It doesn't surprise me that meth is popular in these po-dunk towns," he says. "As shipping becomes global, the drug has gone everywhere."

He's absolutely right. Relatively small amounts of precursor chemicals and lab equipment are now available to everyone by way of international shipping services. Tiny companies consisting of just one or two people tucked away in crowded neighborhoods of places like East Berline, Calcutta, Bangkok, or Jakarta, are able to act as global wholesalers for things that can no longer be easily acquired through traditional outlets in the United States. The chemist in the U.S. only needs this domestic retail contact, and he is in business.

According to Stanton, the phenomenon is in some respects beginning to look more like traditional drug commerce. "In some cases the entire process is being outsourced, moved outside the country to, say, India where law enforcement is next to nonexistent." It's then smuggled into the United States like any other illegal drug. The approach, however, fails to capitalize on meth's inherent ability to be transported in its component parts, and then synthesized, thereby diminishing the legal liability of its purveyors.

Stanton sees this conventional mode of smuggling as the direct result of more comprehensive drug laws in general, precursor laws in particular, and stiffer penalties for both. Such laws and penalties, he believes, have an unintended consequence. "I see people moving away from conventional drugs and moving toward the most basic and most catastrophic methods, such as inhalants."

This is an observation that, according to Stanton, gives sites like totse.com their reason for being. As bad as drugs like methamphetamine might be, there are worse alternatives to getting high. His logic proceeds along the line that drug laws inhibit users from getting high by relatively safe means, and cause them to get high by the most basic and dangerous, "such as sniffing glue and fumes from a can of spray paint. You're never going to be able to stop that. You can't stop people from getting high." Hence, the Temple of the Screaming Electron, where anyone can learn everything about any synthesis. Those who sniff glue need no instruction, no totse.com.

Nearly every day Stanton and Hunter receive messages from "concerned citizens" asking and sometimes demanding that they take the methamphetamine recipes down from their website. "Our response to that is always the same," Stanton says. "'Sorry, but we can't help you.'" He and his coadministrator see the website as a forum for free expression of every order. It is a view held in quarters one might not expect. Surely it's worth noting that never has anyone at totse.com been contacted by law enforcement concerning its content.

According to the DEA's Rogene Waite, Stanton and Hunter have little to fear. "Like all of us, they're protected by the First Amendment," she says. "Unless they break the law, they won't be prosecuted."

And she's right. To break the law one must either make that first molecule of methamphetamine, or show intent to do so. Merely posting recipes on the internet doesn't qualify.

But not all law enforcement entities view the First Amendment through the same lens. In March of 2001 police raided a home in a Denver, Colorado trailer park owned by a man suspected of manufacturing methamphetamine. In the course of their search they found two recipe books on how to make the drug, along with an invoice from the Tattered Cover bookstore.

The next day two plainclothes police officers arrived at the bookstore with a search warrant. They wanted to know if books by an author who writes under the colorful pseudonym Uncle Fester had been purchased by the suspect. The books they were interested in are entitled *Secrets of Methamphetamine Manufacture*, and *Advanced Techniques of Clandestine Psychedelic Drug Laboratories*. The officers claimed the identity of the buyer of the two books was critical to their case. The store balked, refusing to surrender the information on First Amendment grounds, which set the stage for a landmark court battle.

At a subsequent hearing a Colorado court upheld the police request, a decision that owner of the Tattered Cover, Joyce Meskis challenged in the Colorado Supreme Court. "It's not our job to do the police's work for them," she explained to the swelling ranks of media.

The Tattered Cover's general manager, Matthew Miller, was also in the middle of the action. "Our stance was based on the issue of protecting privacy," he says. "We certainly were not trying to prevent the police from doing their job."

The case quickly piqued nationwide interest, and brought out support from literary heavyweights such as Michael Chabon, David Eggers and Dorothy Allison. Fundraisers were held for the bookstore's defense, and later that year Meskis and Miller were rewarded for their stand when the Colorado Supreme Court overturned the previous judge's ruling on the matter, handing down a unanimous six-zero decision in the bookstore's favor.

In the end there is a final irony to the legendary legal battle. The defendant was prosecuted and found guilty, but there was a bit of information known only to a handful of people at the Tattered Cover—information that would not have advanced the government's case against the defendant whatsoever.

"What only a few of us knew at the time," Miller now explains, "was that he never bought those books from us."

The legal fees, he concedes, were tremendous. Thus J.C. Stanton may have some reasons to worry about government interference after all. State and local entities don't seem as concerned with Constitutional niceties as the Feds.

Stanton is also accurate in his understanding of methamphetamine's popularity in the gay community. This niche market for meth sprang into the public consciousness during the summer of 1997, with the murder of five people, followed by a suicide.

Today Andrew Cunanan is known most widely as the young man who murdered Gianni Versace. Cunanan was a familiar face in the gay communities of

San Diego and San Francisco. He was also heavily into crystal meth, which had become commonplace in many gay circles. As some of those who knew him well claim, the five people he murdered and his own suicide were the result of amphetamine psychosis.

Maureen Orth's book *Vulgar Favors* (Dell, 1999) not only chronicles the course of Cunanan's desperation but establishes its root causes. In it she quotes Vance Coukoulis, an acquaintance of Cunanan's, concerning his crystal habit: "It's a sex drug, and all it does is just heighten your whole sexual feeling about a million times." He also adds that "It makes you think about sex twenty-four hours a day. The whole system's become so promiscuous it's frightening. I believed in the devil after I got involved with the gay society and crystal meth, and then I realized evil existed in human nature and that human nature can be of good or of evil, and I really believe in evil now. Period. And I believe an evil spirit can overtake people, and I believe that's what happened to Andrew. He changed through the use of that drug."

For three months during the summer of 1997 Cunanan ran wild on a cross-country killing spree, murdering Jeffrey Trail and David Madson, two former lovers, as well as Lee Miglin, a Chicago real estate magnate, and William Reese, whom Cunanan killed for his truck. Cunanan then drove to Florida where he waited outside Gianni Versace's home. As Versace was walking in on July 15, 1997 Cunanan fired two shots into the back of Versace's head, killing him. Eight days later Cunanan was found dead on a houseboat after having shot himself in the mouth.

Cunanan seemed to enjoy killing. One of his victims had had his head wrapped in duct tape, and was then stabbed in the chest with pruning sheers. After being severely beaten, the man's throat was then cut with a hack saw. Finally, the body was driven over again and again until it was, in the words of one law enforcement officer, "mush." Herein, it would seem, lay the essence of the weird violence surrounding the world of methamphetamine.

Cunanan has been diagnosed posthumously as a narcissist, someone who has a grandiose sense of self-importance, believes they are "special," and is preoccupied with fantasies of unlimited success. They also require unlimited admiration, are themselves arrogant, and most significantly, lack feelings of empathy.[1] Heavy methamphetamine use naturally reinforces these feelings, heightening the narcissist's aggrandized vision of himself, and discounting the feelings those around

---

1.   *Diagnostic and Statistical Manual of Mental Disorders*, Fourth Edition, 1996, American Psychiatric Association

him. Under the influence of meth, such unstable personalities become murderously explosive.

The same is true for those with Borderline Personality Disorder (BPD), for they typically display a wide range of impulsive behaviors that are often self-destructive. They are unstable emotionally, and show wide mood swings in response to stressful events. Brief psychotic episodes are not uncommon. Interestingly, research suggests that the condition may be associated with decreased serotonin levels in the brain, one of the neurotransmitters Ecstasy toys with...hence the uncommon allure.

29

The published facts surrounding the arrest of Clyde Pierson read like an episode of COPS. According to the local paper Clyde and an unidentified woman were sitting at a Sonic Burger restaurant near College Station when the pair began to argue. Suddenly the woman lifted the bun of a cheeseburger and pressed the cheeseburger into Clyde's face. He retaliated by dumping diet Coke over her head. The manager finally called the police once the woman had wrestled Clyde to the floor and appeared to be having some success in her bid to scratch his eyes out.

When police arrived Clyde fought himself free of the woman and bolted for the door. But it was too late for Clyde. Once cuffed, he gave police a name other than what was on his driver's license. It didn't take long for the officer to learn of the warrant out for Clyde's arrest. Bail, the story concluded, had been set at $300,000.

I carefully fold the paper and set it on the kitchen table. Without smiling I hear myself say aloud, "Very funny story."

Later that afternoon Lucille calls to tell me she can be reached at her mother's and stepfather's for the foreseeable future.

"That's as good a place as any for you," I say. "By the way, I read about you and Clyde in the paper this morning."

"I have no idea what you're talking about."

"Didn't think you would."

"I'll need to move the rest of my things out of the house."

And that, I am to assume, is that. From here on out it shall be all documents and lawyers.

A long silence is filled with the thud of my heart in my ears.

"Come back, Lucille."

Her reply is an audible squeak. Tears, I know, are now streaming down the channels of her face into her mouth.

"Come back and we'll be a family."

The squeak becomes a squeal.

"We're both too old for this shit. Come on, Lucille…"

Her sinuses are voided in a tremendous din, and then we merely sit on the line, listening to the slowing cadence of her breathing. A handful of seconds later she says quite soberly, "Sterling, I'm such a wreck."

"Come back."

"This whole thing's insane…How can you want me back?"

"I knew you as a little girl, Lucille."

She tries to speak but can't.

"Walk away from him. At some point you have to."

"Why are you saying this?"

"You're innocent, Lucille…and Clyde is death."

◆   ◆   ◆

That night Colette comes by the ranch with a copy of the day's paper. As I lead her through the gate and into the house she laughs with a forced air of triumph.

"Once he makes bail I'm sure they'll find plenty of reasons to make up," she says with a grimace. A moment later, however, she's not smiling. Her eyes glisten with something else.

"You okay?" I ask.

She nods and then deflects any notions of self-pity with the wave of a hand. "Things are tough all over," she says.

"They are."

What I don't say is that within a few hours I'll be committing high treason in our little coalition of the brokenhearted. In a little while I'll be sleeping with the enemy.

"You really think Clyde can make bail?" I ask.

"To bond out he'd have to come up with ten percent of three-hundred grand. Clyde doesn't know anybody with that kind of money—except you."

Then I can assure you he's not making bail, I want to tell her. But my treasonous mind is bent on rationalizations based on bitter reality. Your husband is more guilty than my wife. He will sleep with the wolves, with his own kind, while my wife sleeps in my own warm bed. Our life will pick up where it left off, while yours tapers into loneliness, poverty and despair. Such is the subtext of what I feel, so I refrain from explaining myself at all.

Instead, I mix a couple of drinks, and we head out to the backyard. Through the next hour I come to realize that Clyde's incarceration isn't the flawless case of justice that I like to think it is. Suddenly Colette is left with four children and no means of support; her family has been torn asunder. Before the arrest Clyde was at least good for a paycheck—be it from ranching, driving a Cat, or manufacturing methamphetamine. It was money. Under normal conditions I am convinced Colette is unerringly good and sound of judgment. What I once took for the personality of a biddy was but an expression of motherly anxiety. In a moment of candor I tell her that she and Clyde just don't add up. The comment is meant to impart an apology for the shoddy treatment I initially inflicted. It's also an appeal to her confidence in who she is without her crackpot husband at her side.

"I've heard it all before," she says. Her only other comment is that "Clyde hasn't always been paranoid and ugly."

"Was there a magic moment in your courtship where you looked at him and said to yourself, 'Oh, yeah. He's the one'?"

Colette's gaze turns fierce. "I think you don't want to admit that Lucille broke your heart."

I ascent to a degree with a groan. "My ego is outraged."

In time the conversation peters out. Colette drives off in her beat up car, and I head back inside to await her imminent disapproval and outrage. So I've made a separate peace. So allies become enemies.

The following day I drive to Lucille's mother's house in Houston where I find Lucille in a cotton summer dress. Pregnancy becomes her. She has regained some of her weight, as her limbs have shed their wasted appearance, and her tummy stands out with a faint, healthy crown. Meeting her on the porch steps, she turns her cheek to accept a small kiss, her gaze always averted to prevent a meeting of eyes. I am denied a smile—her way, I suppose, of insisting that she be allowed to return on her own terms and without conditions. If I want her back, forgetfulness will be required, memories of the last few months forbidden.

She heads back inside and momentarily returns with a pitifully small box of effects, such as a pair of shoes, a hairbrush, framed pictures of Emily and her extended family. Emily, Lucille explains, is at the zoo with her grandmother. As we drive off, I ask her if she needs some maternity clothes. She nods, and then our eyes meet for the first time.

Life resumes with a new sense of serenity, a part of which is attributable to my decision to stop drinking cold turkey. So out goes the lovely vodka in a clear cold stream down the kitchen sink. The rest of the credit lay with Lucille. I return to work and come home in the evening to a dinner she has prepared with some care. Bills are paid, errands run, appointments with the OBGYN kept. Emily is dropped off and picked up from school. Lucille decides to forego rehab, for, as she puts it, she knows what she needs to do, understands what her life must become and forever remain. Time would seem to prove her right, as she seems to be undergoing a fundamental transformation, a sea change that is difficult to qualify or characterize. Her movements about the house become slow and fluid, her eyes gradually take on a new clarity. At times she seems preoccupied. I try to allow her these private moments, unfettered by someone asking her what she's thinking. Sex is infrequent and lacking the former vigor and enthusiasm, and sometimes I note an element of sadness in Lucille's general comportment, even a kind of boredom with this routine she has so abruptly fallen into. But she seems to have arrived at the realization that this is the way adjusted people live, that we are all at best mildly unhappy, that human existence is not an uninterrupted series of incredible highs and lows. Life is dull but bearable and sustainable. All that's required of her is that she display a clear desire to consolidate her life, and I'm inclined to think she does. What she wants is what she now has: a home, a child, a husband, family and a small circle of friends—a life full of constants and routines. But even everyday life can be touched by the bizarre, the sober analogue of Lucille's crazy meth world. Looking back, one such event is a perfect analogue, outlining what came before and foreshadowing what was to come.

One evening in early September Lucille sits out on the patio under a light listlessly reading a magazine on the lives of fascinating people we see on television and at the movies. As I walk toward her, a glass of iced tea in each hand, a terrific weight falls on my right shoulder, the naked tail of a rat whips across my nose and cheeks.

With a single involuntary spasm I throw the glasses to the ground and tear the rat from my face, though its teeth and tiny clawed feet have burrowed into the side of my upper neck. Lucille screams and runs to the door while I take a broomstick and rap the filthy rodent over the head. The rat snarls as it backs into a corner where it squats under a palmetto. Another rap on the head and it lies still.

I come inside with an acute case of the creeps whereupon Lucille notices I'm bleeding. She leads me straight away to the bathroom where I see the small wounds, tiny punctures that cause me to shutter when I think of how I got them.

Lucille cleans and dresses the wounds with professional tidiness, and we go on with our lives as though the episode never occurred. It is, quite simply, too unpleasant to dwell on for the briefest moment. I just want to forget, to eradicate from memory the ugliness of what happened.

Two weeks later, however, I'm alone at the ranch clearing brush when I come down with a low-grade fever. Soon my neck begins to swell, and I call Lucille, who reminds me of the rat bites. So thoroughly have I forgotten the episode that there is a sense of sudden revelation, a genuine *ah-ha!* moment. She orders me home and drives me directly the hospital where I'm quarantined and placed on large doses of antibiotics. The infection has slowly spread from my neck down to my parotid gland, and now threatens to overwhelm my immune system entirely.

For the next few days Lucille keeps me in her charge, bringing me meals, books, flowers, whatever would make me recover more quickly. Four days later I am discharged, and my quiet and rather solitary life returns to the familiar, comfortable pattern. But small events can cast tremendous shadows.

On my first day back at work Colette calls me at the office. My voice is tentative as I tell her about the revised state of my affairs. No apologies, no condolences are necessary. She actually heard about it some time ago. She's happy for me, or at least hopeful that all will come around, that all will be made right. Maybe Lucille can be rehabilitated. Maybe not, but then again, maybe. To change the subject I tell her about my encounter with the rat, and she screams with horrified delight. She's happy that I've recovered. Then it's time to say goodbye.

"I hope you have a good life," she says wistfully. "You deserve one."

"You as well, Colette."

And so my life with Lucille resumes. And so it resumes…

Six weeks before Lucille's due date I am at the check-out counter of a grocery store when the clerk hands me back my debit card.

"This isn't going through," she says.

"There should be several thousand dollars in there," I say handing it back. "Try it again."

She does, but with the same result. For the first time in my life I buy groceries on a credit card.

On my way out to the car I put a call in to the bank to check the balance, and sure enough I'm overdrawn. With the bank officer on the phone I instruct her to transfer seven thousand from savings over to checking. After giving her the account number there's a long silence that says it all. "Either you or your wife drew against the entire balance of both accounts," the voice sweetly croons.

"When did this happen?" I ask.

"Most of the activity occurred…yesterday."

When I come home Lucille and Emily are gone. I drop by the post office and put a series of calls in to the various institutions. A sense of panic suddenly develops as I learn that every account with Lucille's name on it has been cleaned out; a small account with only my name on it has been left untouched. The post office box is stuffed with credit card statements from Neiman Marcus, Kohl's, a top-drawer furniture store. The Visas and MasterCards in her name are maxed at tens of thousands each. I call Lucille's mother to find out if she has seen her daughter.

"She dropped Emily off this morning," she says. "Said she had to leave town for a while."

"Did she say where she was going?"

"Nope."

Evidently she has nothing more to say on the matter, and so she simply hangs up.

Lucille, it would seem, is just gone. She doesn't come home that night or the following day. Later that week Colette calls me in Houston. Her voice is hesitant.

"Clyde made bail."

The moment is lost to this all-consuming thought until I hear Colette saying my name.

"Sterling? You there?"

"I think I know where the money came from," I say.

"Clyde's always been able to sniff out money—even from jail. Wow. I told you he's good."

"I'm feeling pretty stupid and vulnerable right about now, Colette."

"You should probably be feeling a little scared too."

"Have you heard from him?"

"Grapevine has it that he's looking for whoever he thinks put him in jail."

"Tell him it's the same person who got him out."

"Clyde keeps his own score," she says. "Does Lucille have a key to your house?"

"She does."

"Then I'm sure he's already been in there."

"Lucille wouldn't let him in, Colette."

"If the pile of crystal was big enough she would."

"She doesn't want to see me dead."

"But Clyde does, and he has something your wife wants very badly."

The conversation ends with some gentle accusations, and I hang up in my silent office, muttering, "She wouldn't give him the key."

Nevertheless, I find myself moving about the house, into each room, looking under every bed, in each closet, every tub. But I feel no better for the search. I head for my office and collapse on a swivel chair, thinking, this is not the direction I thought my life would be heading as I approached forty…Then something catches my eye. Leaning back, I see what looks like a strip of duct tape coursing down the inside of the desk to the floor. I get down on all fours, and there I see a baby monitor taped to the top of the leg space under the desk. The AC adapter cable has been taped to the interior wall leading down to the computer's surge protector. I turn onto my back so that I'm looking up at the monitor with its little plastic-encased transmitter antenna, the innocent primary colors of its manufacturer's logo.

"That you, Clyde?" I whisper. "Waiting for me to fall asleep?"

I get up and walk over to the office window where I see a ladder extending up from the ground. The window itself has been unlocked. I sit back down and consider the intellectual wherewithal of my opponent; then I consider what he came here to do, and my blood runs cold.

"So you want me dead, Lucille?" I shout into the rafters. *"Is that what you want?"*

So sleep is warded away. At four in the morning the phone rings. My eyes open at the command of adrenaline. I find myself in my swivel chair before my desk, the lights on. I allow myself a moment to take a reading of my own mind, and then very slowly lift the receiver. Clyde's nasal breath fills the connection. After a long silent interval, he says in a singing voice, "That's what she wants, Mr. Braswell!" With that thought conveyed he hangs up, and for the balance of the night his sleepless world is mine.

30

Today amphetamines and methamphetamine are more prevalent than ever in spite of a crush of new legislation and special attention lavished on the problem by law enforcement. The last set of federal laws to come down the pike came in the form of the Methamphetamine Anti-Proliferation Act of 2000 (MAPA), which addresses the fundamentals of clandestine production. Cold medicines that didn't come in blister packs would have their potency dramatically reduced. Perhaps of greater significance, the Act addressed the discrepancy in penalties for those caught with large amounts of precursor chemicals and those caught with the finished product. If it looks like you're about to make methamphetamine, then, in the eyes of the law, you've made methamphetamine.

Ironically, much of the news today concerning the molecule has to do with the few remaining legal and "legitimate" applications. The most contentious example is the case of methylphenidate, the drug more commonly known by its trade name, Ritalin. What isn't so widely known is that Ritalin's molecular structure has an "amphetamine backbone," and produces an effect similar to that of amphetamine and methamphetamine. As such, it has been listed as a Schedule II drug. Perhaps most surprising of all in light of these facts is that Ritalin is chiefly prescribed to adolescent children for attention deficit disorder (ADD), and attention deficit and hyperactivity disorder (ADHD).

The drug's popularity has skyrocketed in recent years, alarming some in the medical field, educators, and parents, creating something of a backlash. Children who take it are often said to be zombies, the parents who allow it intolerant of typical unruly behavior. The doctors who prescribe it must then be corrupted by the pharmaceutical industry. One of the Columbine shooters is widely rumored to have been on Ritalin.

But the controversy hasn't quashed the drugs popularity. Figures published in an article in "Forbes" magazine in 1996 indicated a four-fold increase in the rate of Ritalin consumption in the five years from 1989 to 1994. Indeed the trend has only reinforced itself. Two years later the United Nations released a report that claimed ten to twelve percent of all male school children in the United States were taking the drug. According to the National Institute of Mental Health approximately three to five percent of the population has either of the disorders.

In prescribed doses Ritalin's effect on children with ADHD has a calming effect, allowing them to focus their attention more readily. But in adults it behaves more like old fashioned amphetamine, and as a result a disturbing trend has recently developed with parents taking their children's Ritalin. Some have even tried dissolving the tablets in water in order to inject the drug as they would methamphetamine. The result is most unpleasant. The insoluble fillers used in the tablets block small blood vessels, causing painful damage to the lungs and retina of the eye.

Ritalin has found a home in professional sports as well, especially baseball. Yankee's pitcher David Wells claims that some major leaguers use the drug for its stimulant properties. An even more commonplace substance in baseball, however, is ephedra, the over-the-counter amphetamine-like herbal supplement that has many of the same characteristics.

On February 16, 2003, Baltimore Orioles pitcher Steven Bechler showed up for a spring training workout in Fort Lauderdale. Within a few hours he collapsed in the Florida heat. His temperature spiked to 108 degrees, at which point his organs began to fail. The following day he died. The heatstroke, it is believed, was in part brought on by the pitcher's use of ephedra, a dietary supplement containing ephedrine.

Bechler had been taking the supplement in order to lose weight, a problem he had wrestled with all his life. Although it had been banned by the NCAA, the NFL, and the International Olympic Committee, it's still permitted in major league baseball. With Bechler's death the Food and Drug Administration (FDA) moved to require the products to bear warning labels that ephedra can cause heart attack and stroke. The news hit the ephedra industry hard. The Nutrition Business Journal estimated that $1.3 billion worth of supplements containing ephedra were sold in the United States in 2002; the following year's totals came to a mere $500 million. Although there have been reports of at least 155 deaths linked to ephedra use, for years the FDA claimed it didn't have proof that it is sufficiently dangerous to be brought under strict federal regulation—a result of the dietary supplement industry's successful lobbying efforts. The American Medical Association has felt differently about ephedra, favoring, as they have, an outright ban of the product. In the spring of 2004 the FDA abruptly changed course and followed suit, finally instituting just such a ban.

The real perception problem for the government concerning amphetamine lay in the military application of the drug. This dramatically came to light in the night skies over Afghanistan on April 18, 2002. The little known but longstanding use of amphetamine in the form of Dexedrine made headlines when two U.S.

Air Force F-16 pilots, Majors Harry Schmidt and William Umbach of the Illinois Air National Guard, saw flashes on the ground and thought they were being fired upon.

The tragedy unfolded with an air of arrogance and incompetence. Initially, Schmidt asked permission to unload cannon fire on the target, but was told to hold fire until the target could be identified as friendly or hostile by AWACS planes in the area. A few minutes later Schmidt abruptly declared "self-defense," and pealed off.

The rules of engagement require that pilots wait for clearance. Schmidt, however, simply went ahead and acted on a hunch, dropping a 227-kilogram laser-guided bomb. Thirty-eight seconds later the AWACS patrol came back with the devastating conclusion that they had just bombed friendlies; Canadian forces were currently on the ground conducting live-fire exercises on the ground. Four soldiers of the Edmonton-based Alpha Company, 3rd Battalion, Princess Patricia's Canadian Light Infantry had been killed, and eight wounded.

To the shock of the American and Canadian publics, it was learned that the pilots were on amphetamines in the form of Dexedrine that night. Moreover, the pilots claimed they felt obligated to take them. Were they to decline they felt they might be scrubbed from the mission. The amphetamines, they said, impaired their judgment, making them impatient and overly aggressive. The aggression, the U.S. government countered in its case against the pilots, was more of the order of "failure to exercise appropriate flight discipline."

Air Force guidelines generally clear pilots for amphetamine use on any mission over eight hours in duration. Schmidt's and Umbach's mission was to last fourteen, so they were not only free to use Dexedrine, but, as they claim, they felt *compelled* to do so. In fact, amphetamine use is something of an open secret in the Air Force. In Desert Storm, for instance, a full two-thirds of the aviators used amphetamines during their deployment. Sixty percent of them said it was "essential" to their mission.

At first glance the pilots' story might seem reasonable. But as the background of the circumstances came into relief, another story emerged. This came in the form a report produced jointly by Brig.-Gen. Stephen T. Sargeant of the U.S. Air Force and Canadian Brig.-Gen. Marc Dumais. By their lights the tragedy had very little to do with Dexedrine.

According to the report the doses were tiny. Umbach had taken 5-milligram "go pill" two hours before the accident, and Schmidt a 10-mg just an hour before—doses which would be similar to drinking a few cups of strong coffee (the DEA, by comparison, has cited speed freaks who have injected several hundred milligrams of methamphetamine in a single sitting). The pills are hardly potent enough to produce the kind of amphetamine psychosis their defense suggested. When the personal dynamics between the two pilots were revealed, a more plausible story came into focus.

The report claims that Major Umbach was known as an "average pilot," whereas Schmidt was a much decorated Top Gun flight school instructor, and was nicknamed "Psycho" by his fellow pilots. Unfortunately Umbach was the flight commander that night, and Schmidt is noted for having little regard for Umbach, which led to a critical breakdown in flight discipline.

The rules of engagement in Afghanistan dictated that it was the commander's job to order Schmidt to take normal defensive action that night by simply flying out of harms way until he received clearance to drop the bomb. Incredibly, it typically takes but five minutes for AWACS planes to investigate such sightings and either grant or deny clearance to attack what is suspected to be an enemy ground position; Schmidt waited only two minutes before dropping the laser-guided bomb. In the end both pilots were brought up on bad conduct discharges, with Schmidt also being charged with failing to exercise appropriate flight discipline, and failure to comply with the rules of engagement.

The tragedy's broader impact has to do with the military's use of "go pills" and "no-go pills," the latter of which they use today in the form of zolpidem (Ambien) and temazepam (Restoril). And yet the military may soon be writing off amphetamines for good—but not because they find them ineffective or detrimental to a pilot's or soldier's judgment. Rather, they have found something superior. A new class of drugs has appeared on the horizon called "eugeroics," which merely means "good arousal." The FDA recently approved modafinil, one of two eugeroic drugs, to treat narcolepsy, which has been typically treated with Dexedrine. What modafinil does is boost wakefulness by aping the brain chemistry of a well rested person.

The need for such drugs in the Air Force is pretty straight-forward: sleep deprived pilots make more mistakes. But so too do pilots with amphetamine-induced jitters. Modafinil causes wakefulness, but unlike amphetamines, it doesn't produce hyperactivity in the form of the shakes. Research conducted by the U.S. Army has shown pilots on modafinil have been able to fly two forty-hour missions, separated by only one night of sleep. Their performance was roughly on par with that of fully rested pilots for the eighty-hour duration. Modafinil has also shown itself to be remarkably nonaddicting, working as it does with a tiny number of neurotransmitters in the hypothalamus called Norepinephrine, the very wheels and gears of our body clock. Where amphetamines wake up the brain as a whole, modafinil is extremely specific. The drug may prove so revolutionary that some have speculated advances in such drugs could make sleep unnecessary.

But modafinil is very complex, and amphetamine and methamphetamine very simple. They, or something very much like them, will be with us forever. The addict is in pursuit of euphoria, something modafinil doesn't deliver. Mother Nature Herself has made it so tantalizingly easy for us. And so has Progress, which, it can be argued, has delivered western civilization to the brink of mass annihilation and madness.

The unguarded proliferation of information and technology has lent the world a new combustibility, for ours is an age of the super-empowered individual. Given a few minutes, one can find instructions on how to build a nuclear device, develop a colony of anthrax, or make vast amounts of powerful drugs in your bathtub. For the first time in human history the individual has it within his reach to wreak catastrophe across large swaths of human populations. The brave new world is a dangerous new world, and the methamphetamine phenomenon is its soul.

31

Late in the afternoon a lady officer from the Houston P.D. drops by the house. At first she seems interested in my story. But in the course of the telling I mention that I'm getting a divorce. With these words the pen and notepad are discreetly tucked away. She'll try to remember everything I say.

Staring at the notepad in her pocket, I point out that a big time methamphetamine chemist I had arrested is now out on bond. He has made repeated threats against my life. He has broken into my house and installed an eavesdropping device. The officer smiles. It's all part of a nasty divorce and the listening device is a baby monitor. Boiled down to law enforcement argot, "It's a civil matter which means there isn't much we can do."

"Breaking and entering isn't a civil matter," I say.

"He used your wife's key, right? So there was no 'breaking,'" she says, four fingers clawing in the air for quotes. Need she say more? No, she needn't. "A detective will be getting in touch with you tomorrow," she says on her way out. "Maybe a restraining order or even a protective order would be appropriate."

But the next day no one from the Houston P.D. calls, no one comes by. If my brains are dashed away in my sleep, I ask myself, will it be the same anemic police force investigating my demise?

Clyde, I learn in the meantime, has a real gift for terror. He lets me know he's been lurking about in subtle yet unmistakable ways—a necktie hanging from the rearview mirror in my locked car, the end of the tie lopped off...a rifle target of a human silhouette taped to the front door of my house. Coming home from work one day I find on the foyer floor a Polaroid of my wife at the height of her chemical madness. In the photo she wears camo-fatigues and aims a high-powered rifle at one of the human targets on the ranch. The picture is dated, I note, as Lucille is not showing. She stands before the dam on the ranch in profile, resolute, enraged and horribly skinny—Clyde's first lieutenant in his lunatic militia. He wants me to know that my world has turned against me because I have turned against him, that he can do whatever he wants whenever he wants, that I am at the mercy of a madman and his mad girlfriend, whom he has recruited to his way of thinking and who happens to be my wife. On each of these scores, I must admit, he is correct. He is also effective.

The effect on me is not merely psychological but physical. Upon waking up on a warm December morning I am suddenly taken by an overwhelming lethargy. It's more than ordinary fatigue, as my vision is tunnel-like, and I feel a general numbness in my extremities. As I get out of bed and head for the shower, I sense that I'm not a part of my immediate surroundings; it's as though reality itself is somehow surreal, the edges blurred, the colors washed away. Tactile sensation is eerily vague.

I call work to tell them I won't be in, and head straight for the doctor's office where a nurse takes my temperature and checks my blood pressure. The first blood pressure reading is "ridiculously high," almost higher than she's ever seen. So she takes another. Her eyelashes flutter as she pulls her stethoscope from her ears. "Mr. Braswell," she says, "your blood pressure is…190 over 160…"

The doctor comes in, takes a reading himself, and immediately orders a drug regimen that includes a beta blocker, a calcium channel blockers and an ace inhibitor. After a few more tests he discovers that I am in the midst of renal failure. Dialysis certainly lies in my future, and possibly a kidney transplant. The hospital shall be my home away from home from this day forward.

"What's going on with you, Sterling?" he says as he pushes himself away from my table on his wheeled stool. Unlike the Houston P.D., he would seem to be deeply curious.

"It's a long, sad story, doc," I say.

"Let's hear it."

And so I begin, condensing the entirety down to a minute or so. When I finish, he appears stricken. My heart instantly attaches itself to this busy old man who recognizes a well-spent two minutes. Suddenly I feel as though I am about to break down, begin crying uncontrollably. The doctor's expression seems to suggest that this might be a good thing.

I feel the tears rise up, crest, then subside. Don't want to head down that path. Once I do there will be no end to it.

"You need to get out of Houston," he murmurs. "If your wife's crazy associates don't kill you, the stress of the situation will."

"Unfortunately a living must be made—or, in my case, remade," I say.

He shakes his head. "There is no living to be made if you're not alive."

"I have a gun."

"Oh, my," he groans. "I don't see this ending happily."

While lying awake in my hospital bed a few nights later the phone rings just before midnight. Lucille's mother informs me that I am the father of a baby girl.

"Eight pounds, nine ounces," she says. "Perfectly healthy, perfectly content. Lucille calls her 'Maria.'" Click.

Ambivalence leavens the reflex of joy. It occurs to me that a paternity test should be done, but then I realize I want the child whether or not she's mine. In the meantime I'm discharged from the hospital. My strength isn't entirely back, and I feel frail in a most general sense, like my kidneys are held together by strands of glass. Three days later there's a knock at the door. I thrust myself to my feet and hobble down the stairs in my bathrobe. Lucille's mother stands in the doorway with the baby tightly wrapped in a blanket like a burrito.

"Looks like I gotta raise one of my grandchildren all by myself now," she yaps as she hands over little Maria, "*and I'm too old to be-a raisin' another!*"

"Can't say I blame you," I remark.

"Better get some diapers and formula," she says before strutting off for the Lexus that was once mine, then her daughter's, and now, apparently, hers.

I look down at the tiny sleeping eyes, feel the ghostly weight in my arms. There's no doubt the girl is mine.

"Welcome to planet Earth, Maria," I whisper as I pet her faint pale hair. "My name is Sterling, and my life is a mess."

Perhaps it is mere ego, or the reality that I've been given something after so much has been stripped away. Maybe it's that overriding instinct of general good cheer indigenous to every new parent that overwhelms even the bleakest circumstance. Whatever it is it delivers a weird, foreign happiness to the place in my brain that was once a simple void. If only I were well, I tell myself. But well or not, Maria is utterly helpless. I make a few phone calls, and soon friends appear as though arriving for a baby shower.

The incoherent childhood, so I've been told, is the germ of the unhappy adult. Looking down on my daughter, this is what I fear most. Her mother is inextricably bound up in both of our lives, and she is all about chaos. But some problems solve themselves, or are at least replaced by new problems.

From early on Lucille makes it clear that childrearing is no longer a natural inclination of hers. In those initial postnatal months she comes by only once. Late one morning there's a sharp knock on the door, and there she stands, grim and furious, here, she says, "to visit her child" if that's all right with me.

All traces of her former tranquility have been vanquished, replaced by jittery rage. She doesn't seem high, yet her eyes are glazed, as though the lenses themselves seek to shield her heart from the sight she's about to behold. She has become another person, an angry victim, furious at what's been done to her, but vague as to just what that is. Her weight enhances her fierce, brittle posture. A month after having given birth she probably weighs a hundred pounds.

I lead Lucille into the nursery where Maria is sleeping, and we look down on her together from either side of the basinet. She extends her bony little finger to Maria's tiny hand, and Maria instinctively takes it in her sleep. Tears tumble over Lucille's cheeks and are instantly absorbed into the bedding. "Your mommy loves you, Maria," she mouths. "Don't ever forget about me…"

She then withdraws her finger, and walks out of the room and out of the house. I follow her outside and call to her as she staggers down the street for her car.

"Where can I find you?" I yell after her.

She turns about, her face streaked with tears and a tangle of black hair, her voice clogged with pure inarticulate emotion. In the absence of her ability to speak, she reaches for the door handle to her car and gets in. On the passenger seat is a handgun, on the floor a propane tank. Seeing that I've noticed, she tries to scream but can't. She scowls. Her teeth are cinch, eyes ablaze. A witchlike middle finger is thrust against the marred window. With that, she's off.

I watch the silver car round the corner. A sheen of white mud gleams in the lateral morning light, lending it the look of a well-traveled rocket ship on its long distance journey into deep space. So Lucille is gone, a solitary traveler on a strange journey to a warring planet of plastic people. Final escape.

Two weeks later a court awards custody of our daughter to me by default, as Lucille fails to show up for the scheduled hearings. But now there is the problem of finances. When the accounting is done, the numbers are staggering. More than a million dollars have been siphoned from various checking and savings accounts, or charged to this or that credit card. Lucille, I discover, has been quietly spiriting away wealth wherever she could find it since having met Clyde. The ranch cannot be sold in its poisoned state, and has several liens against it to boot. The house is put on the market, and my daughter and I move into a small apartment in downtown Houston in a neighborhood populated by lots of friends. The space is spare, ugly and nearly devoid of furniture. I hire a nanny, as I now face the prospect of raising a child without a spouse. But I soon come to realize that I've never been more convinced of my own happiness. I'm sick, stone broke and happy. Lucille is in her spaceship, and I'm bouncing a baby girl on my knee in an empty living room. Granted, a loaded pistol is holstered in the front pocket of my pajamas. The universe can be an infinitely dark and lonely place, yet it can also render what you never thought you needed.

Events fall toward the latter end of this spectrum the following winter when I receive a call from my father.

"Turn on Channel Nine," he says with an uncharacteristic thrill in his voice.

The newscast is in the midst of a local story concerning Clyde Pierson, who has just been arrested in New Mexico. Initially he was pulled over for having expired plates on his car, whereupon a mobile methamphetamine lab was discovered in his vehicle. A cache of automatic weapons and approximately fifty-thousand pseudoephedrine tablets were found in the backseat. His priors are mentioned, which explains the 3.2 million-dollar bail. Lucille's name never comes up, an accomplice never mentioned. Ten percent, I remind myself, is $320,000.

I have to believe we are safe. I hang up and turn off the television. Lucille has surely spent everything she has ever stolen.

In the quiet I reach for the pistol. Perspiration from my hand has discolored the gunmetal in the colors of a dark rainbow. I watch the layer of moisture evaporate from the curved surfaces of the handle, listening all the while to the insistent thud of my heart in my ears I've been living with, a kind of grisly white noise.

Within this relative silence I hear my daughter's soft cry emerge from the bedroom, the voice blossoming from a nap. I pick up the gun, pop the clip, check the empty chamber for a round. So I withdraw from Crazy Town with my daughter and my life, and without my health and wealth. So be it. I reach my hand within the square of the strongbox's interior. Ah, so pleasantly cool. The gun's safety is depressed, the barrel holstered in nylon webbing and locked away with its fully stuffed clip. One never knows. The box's door is closed, the dial spun, and I walk away. Far off in the apartment my daughter purrs. Time to change a diaper. Time to prepare a warm bottle.

That night I drift off to sleep before the blue glow of the television with little Maria in my arms. In the dream her mother is suspended before me in the pool's warm water, lighted from within, everything aquamarine. Lucille's breath floats over the surface in light bursts, smelling of salt water taffy. The boardwalks of Galveston, she says, are all arcades and sweet things to eat. Her shoulders appear burnished in the strange light, almost black from a day at the beach. Life is short, she says. Can't be caught treading water, not for a second. Stop moving and you'll be torn to shreds by sharks. Try and catch me, Sterling. And she dives like a dolphin into the green water, headed directly for the lamp under the diving board, blinding me as I follow. I surface with a gasp, and see her submerged silhouette against the surrounding incandescence. So thin, like an exotic moth or some creature from outer space that is drawn to the furnace of stars. What a strange and pretty picture, I tell myself. So unreal and dream-like.

A great moon hovers overhead, a perfect circle of cold, reflected light. I point it out to Lucille but she doesn't see it. It hangs directly behind her, and she has set a course for the sun.

Epilogue

Given time all disembodied voices in every dream fade, and the cosmos of sharp edges and hard surfaces reemerges. The inevitable is realized, which in turn becomes a history of hard facts and bitter epilogue. Thus it is with Lucille and all those who inhabited her ethereal world.

In the spring of 2002 Clyde was sentenced to eighteen years in state prison. After having been denied access to his laboratory for several contiguous months, he instructed his lawyer to contact my lawyer and tell her that he thinks of me as his brother. He never intended to hurt me.

I happened to be at my lawyer's office when Clyde's idiotic message came through. The television was tuned to a local newscast, and on the screen was a picture of a home in a Houston suburb with a pillar of flame rising through the roof. There before the house was Lucille's car, parked on the street. I interrupted my lawyer and asked her to turn up the volume. Just as I suspected, the story concerned a methamphetamine lab explosion. No deaths were reported, but there were several severe burn injuries. Two neighboring homes were also lost before the conflagration could be put out.

So far Lucille has avoided long-term incarceration, always keeping herself one step ahead of the law. From time to time she would ask to see Maria alone, which I set up through a supervised parental visitation program sponsored by the state. Sometimes Lucille would keep her appointments, but usually not. I haven't seen her in person since she last drove off, but I've been told she is now frail, her health failing. The deeds of the men in her life are casting their final ruin.

Colette is in a relationship with a man who doesn't attend church regularly, but neither does he have a criminal record. She's merely looking for someone who's good, she says—not perfect, not evil. Just good. She's happy with the return of romance in her life, and from time to time she'll get a letter from Clyde. In them he tells Colette that he still thinks of her as his wife. He never intended to hurt her.

Emily now lives with extended family, as her grandmother passed away in the spring of 2003. Maria too is happy and healthy. She began talking at a precociously young age, and often asks about her mother. Does she have one? Where is she? Who is she? My answers are unsatisfying and vague. One day we will meet her, I say. When? she asks. One day. What happened to her? Well…Then my mind sets to work.

Perhaps the story should be told.

978-0-595-38021-3
0-595-38021-2

Made in the USA
Lexington, KY
02 August 2010